THE GOOD LIFE

UP THE YUKON WITHOUT A PADDLE

Dorian Amos

Edited by Caroline Sylge

Published by Eye Books

Copyright © Dorian Amos 2004

All rights reserved. Apart from brief extracts for the purpose of review, no part of this publication may be reproduced, stored in a retrieval system, or transmitted in any form or by any means, electronic, mechanical, photocopying, recording or otherwise without the permission of the publisher.

Dorian Amos has asserted his right under the Copyright, Designs and Patents Act 1988 to be identified as the author of this work.

The Good Life
First Edition
July 2004

Published by Eye Books Ltd
51a Boscombe Rd
London
W12 9HT
Tel/fax: +44 (0) 20 8743 3276
website: www.eye-books.com

Set in Frutiger and Garamond
ISBN: 1903070309

British Library Cataloguing in Publication Data
A catalogue record for this book is available from the British Library

Printed and bound in Great Britain by Biddles Ltd

Cover photograph courtesy of Johnny Caribou, freelance writer and photographer, West Dawson City, who spends too much time at his neighbour Dorian's house.

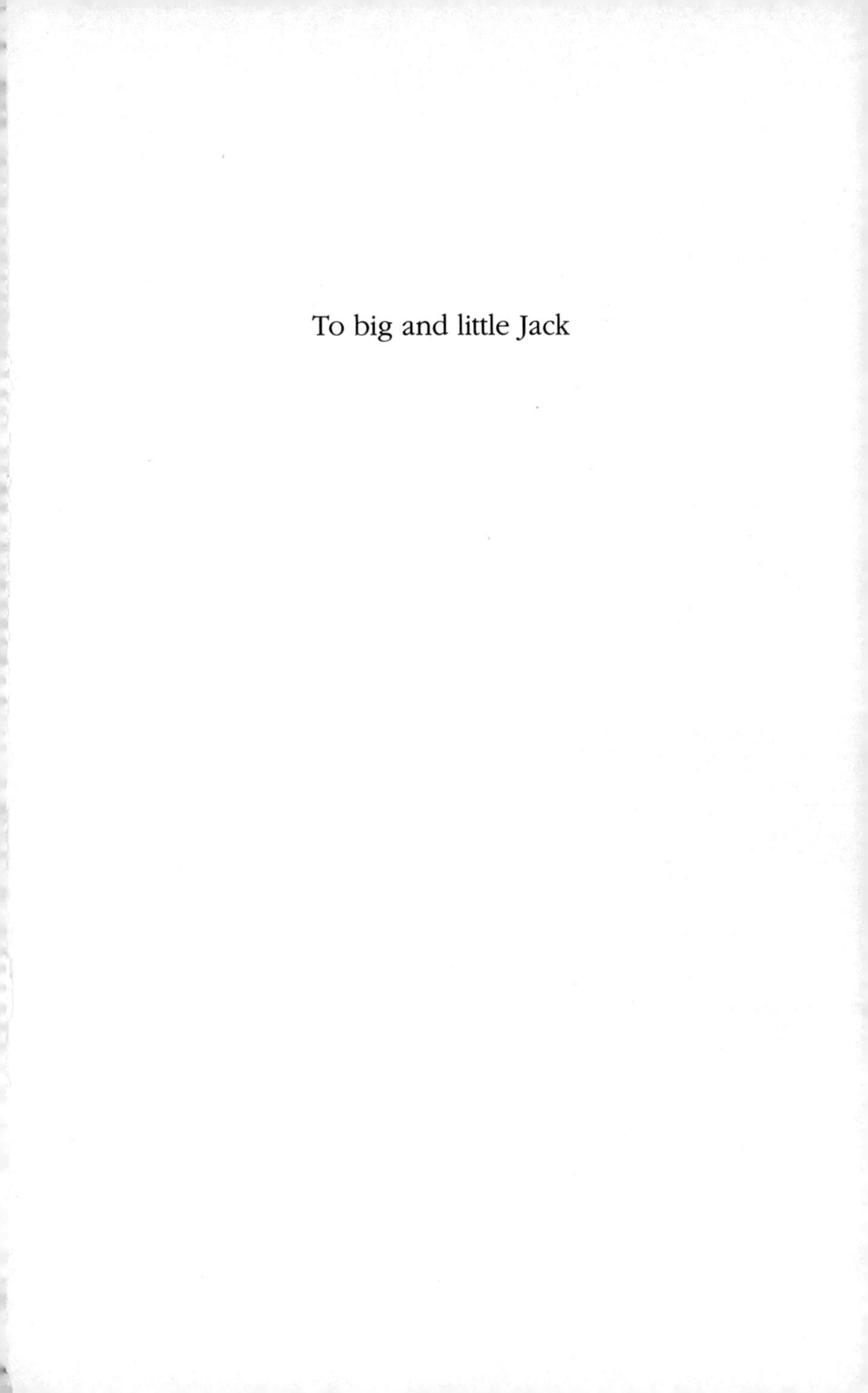

To big and little Jack

Acknowledgments

A fond thank you must go to Matt Lovelock whose help, friendship and dedication smoothed the waves for our immigration across the sea for which I will be forever grateful! To Pam and Glen whose generosity, friendship and support also made a would-be harrowing time seem remarkably comfortable. I'd also like to thank Brent for his endless patience, help and his total acceptance of a dyslexic English cartoonist trying to survive a winter in his neck of the woods.

A big thank you to Carol Mac for her guidance and help. I would also like to thank my parents for somehow, somewhere instilling in me this reckless, full steam ahead approach I have to life, it makes everything so much more interesting. And most of all I'd like to thank Bridget for her unquestioning support and love. She makes everything so worthwhile.

Contents

Foreword

Like moths drawn to the firelight from out of the shadows Dorian and Bridget found themselves sitting around my campfire in Southern England attending a Woodlore Wilderness Bushcraft Course. Already the seed of an adventure had taken root inside of them, but at that time I had no idea of this. With all of the others attending the course they were introduced to the fundamental practicalities of outdoors living. I as the instructor emphasised the value of knowledge over equipment, the importance of perfecting the basic skills and encouraged the class to strive to walk in pace with the rhythms of the wild, rather than trying to over write nature's symphony with our chaotic tempo. If I had known then what Dorian and Bridget had in mind I would certainly have advised further tuition in bushcraft, pointed them at expert canoe coaches and a host of other instructors that would have eased their journey. When I received word of their venture I was cheered but also concerned. Any true tutor wishes nothing more than for their alumni to go out and benefit from their tuition but naturally by dint of the experience necessary to instruct the teacher perhaps appreciates more keenly the risk of such an undertaking.

Dorian and Bridget's adventures have both horrified me and made me laugh, truly ignorance is bliss. It is gratifying to read of their confidence to start a fire in bad weather and the warmth it provided to their morale rises from these pages as though they glow in my hands. But above all else it is their utter determination to break with convention and strike out in search of their dream that warms me the most. In over twenty years teaching bushcraft I have met many who have come to the campfire late in life and regret not having discovered their interest in their youth, and I have taught many times this many who have their youth but not the courage to follow their dreams. It is only a rare handful who dream well and live bravely, they know better than most that, 'Only dead salmon swim with the current'.

Ray Mears
England 2004

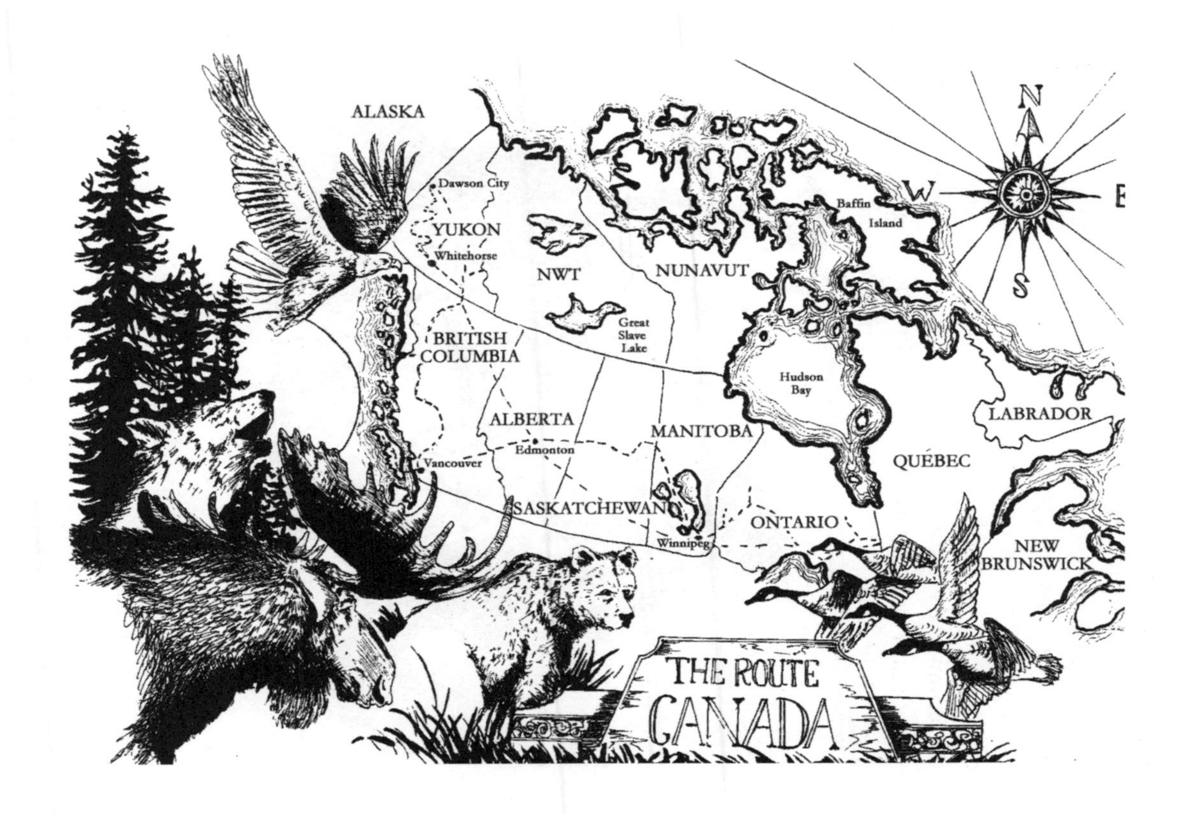
ALASKA
Dawson City
YUKON
Whitehorse
NWT
NUNAVUT
Baffin Island
N
W
E
S
Great Slave Lake
BRITISH COLUMBIA
Hudson Bay
ALBERTA
MANITOBA
LABRADOR
Edmonton
Vancouver
QUÉBEC
SASKATCHEWAN
ONTARIO
Winnipeg
NEW BRUNSWICK
THE ROUTE
CANADA

Part I

January 1998

I was living in Polperro, one of Cornwall's prettiest little fishing villages and friendliest communities. It took me thirty minutes to walk ten yards in the morning to the post office, because everybody wanted to say good morning or talk about fish or the weather. I had my own little business drawing cartoons and selling them in my shop, Amosart. I worked when I wanted, did what I wanted, said what I felt and spent what I liked. There was no struggling to get up in the morning, no commuting in traffic jams or crowded trains, no stress of an over zealous boss breathing down my neck and definitely no sexual harassment. Life wasn't ordinary or boring. Life was pretty good.

It had taken me 5 years to build up my business and create the happy, easy life I had. My wife Bridget had just finished 4 years of university to qualify as a psychiatric nurse. She was now working in a job she loved and we would have an extra 12,000 pounds a year coming in. I was 32, Bridge was 29, and for the first time in our lives money would not be a real problem.

Somehow though, I had started to develop an ache for a little more adventure.

Ignoring the ache, and keeping it to myself, I knuckled down to draw more cartoons. Every morning I'd percolate a pot of coffee, turn up the stereo and draw - until about 3.00 p.m. every day, when my thoughts would begin to wander the world seeking adventure. Soon, I was wandering the world at noon, then 11.00.a.m. until after several months I was fighting crocodiles on the Nile as soon as I sat at the drawing board. My enthusiasm for my work and my business was gone, lost somewhere on the plains of Africa.

May 1998

After 4 months of battling with my dreams I decided one night to talk to Bridge. I watched her as she unwrapped the chips from their soggy paper. She was telling me about her day jabbing backsides with syringes and pushing the panic button because someone had decided they were an aardvark and had started to dig up the carpet with their nose. I wasn't really listening, just watching her gesticulating with the vinegar bottle. Then I heard her sigh, "I'm sick of this shit", and I sat up with heart pounding. "Are you?" I said, "We can make a change you know." Bridge looked at me in a way she had only started to do after qualifying as a psychiatric nurse. I took the plunge and told her about my now overwhelming urge for adventure.

When I'd finished and slumped back into my chair, she said, "If you think about something too much, you just talk yourself out of it and never do it. We're only here once. Let's go get some action! Can you pass the salt please?" And that was it, the decision that would dramatically change our lives.

Bridget returned home the following evening with carrier bags full of travel guides and over the next few days we studied atlases and skimmed through endless books. There was a whole life of adventure to live right there in those pages, but we had no idea where to go - all I knew is that I didn't want to go to the Nile because during my day dreaming a crocodile had rather rudely chewed off my feet.

July 1998

One night my brother Julian phoned. As an officer in the Royal Marines, he's seen action in Bosnia, Somalia and Northern Ireland, and I told him my need for adventure. He listened quietly then said, "I'm on leave next week, which coincides with the running of the bulls in Pamplona - fancy a run?" I accepted immediately and it only occurred to me after I'd put the phone down that he was a lot, lot fitter than I was.

The following Saturday I found myself in the upper deck bar of the six o'clock evening ferry to Spain with a tanned, fit and excited Julian. I, on the other hand, was white, far from fit and coughing on the cigarette I nervously smoked as I contemplated being run over by ten, very large and horny bulls.

My brother had been pretty busy having adventures every day, most of which involved escaping jealous lovers. When he was telling me about his bungy jump in Africa I cut him short with a question. "Does anybody die in the running of the bulls?" He looked at me and laughed, "Are you nervous about this?" "Am I hell!" I snapped in my manly voice. "I just like to know what I'm getting myself into." Julian, knowing I was scared and loving every minute, calmly recited everything he had read about the running of the bulls, including the average number of deaths that occur each year.

The Pamplona festival was like nothing I'd seen before. Music filled the air, and everywhere people were dressed in white and scarlet from head to foot, singing, dancing and drinking shoulder to shoulder. Feeling very welcome we joined them and partied through till 3.00 a.m. when we decided on a short sleep in the Town Square. At 5.30 a.m.

Julian woke me with a Spanish beer. The bars were still rocking, people were still singing and fire-eaters were lighting up the square. Julian jumped to his feet and ordered us to the old town hall for the start of the run.

We climbed over the eight-foot barriers and jumped into the crowded square to stand with masses of drunken men. A chap behind us, who had run yesterday, talked about his experiences, which made several people around us leave with parting words like, "My life is not worth this" and "I'd rather be playing golf." After an hour a loud speaker crackled into life and advised us to run safely, not to hide in doorways and not to stop and help the injured runners. The laughter and singing had stopped as we began to walk up the mile long course. Ahead was a long, extremely narrow street bordered by eight-foot high, heavy wooden barriers. Spectators were piled high around us, clinging to sign posts and drainpipes, cheering from balconies and waving excitedly from windows.

A rocket exploded in the sky behind us, the signal that the first four bulls were out and charging. People started to run, but my brother shouted, "Wait till we see the bulls!" so we stood side by side in the middle of the road as hundreds of people ran around us, pushing to get in front. All I wanted to do was run with the others as fast as I could, why did I have to be here with a hero?

Chaos erupted at the corner fifty feet from us as the bulls charged around it bulldozing runners out of the way. People were literally being hurled into the air as the first four bulls ploughed a path through the runners. Julian turned and shouted every conceivable obscenity loosely linked to 'run'. The crowd was ecstatic as the bulls mowed down the runners behind us. Cries of "Toro! Toro!" filled the air as I

turned and fled, the ground vibrating with the force of the bull's charge.

Before I knew it the first bulls were upon me. I dodged the first one as it pushed and ran over several people. The second bull tripped on the fallen runners and fell right on top of them. I looked for an escape as the bull clambered to its feet, turned and charged back towards me. All I could see were the long sharp horns. My legs felt like lead as I lunged through the runners in a desperate attempt to escape the bull's path. At the last minute it changed track to follow two more bulls as they thundered past. I continued on the run, jumping and scrambling over mounds of fallen runners, before the rest of the bulls caught up with me.

Moments later the stadium was in view. As the course narrowed at the ancient gates, runners were tumbling over each other. I managed to avoid the mess and enter the arena just as the remaining bulls stormed around the corner and through the gates, flattening the fallen men without breaking stride. The crowd roared as the runners spilled into the circular arena followed by the bulls. I'd made it! Everywhere runners hugged each other and danced. The feeling was incredible.

I looked around for my brother and remembered the last time I'd seen him was in the heap of people on the ground in front, dragging a poor Spaniard on top of himself for protection. I headed back down the course to the closest bar. People were lying all over the road, unconscious, limping, being cared for by the paramedics, all of them bleeding from their battered bodies. I pushed through the crowds and ordered the largest beer I could through gesticulation. Twenty minutes later Julian entered the bar, bleeding badly from the elbow but just as high as I was. It was 8.30 in the morning but the night was still young and we had some celebrating to do. This was living!

June 1998

Three days later I was back at my drawing board. It was surprising how quickly I set back into my routine, and it began to worry me. Running the bulls was exciting but short-lived and I was again craving adventure. Bridget and I would talk long into the night about what we wanted out of life. In the words of Henry David Thoreau, we wanted to 'live deliberately'. We also knew we didn't want to work all our lives or have our children (when we had them) grow up thinking money was all there was to life. We wanted to do our best to be happy - and we toasted that thought with the last of our Somerset Scrumpy.

We finally decided on Northern Canada as our destination. It was one of the few untamed wildernesses left in the world, a place full of the adventure and challenges we craved and the freedom to 'live deliberately'. Our great life-changing plan was to emigrate at the end of the summer, buy land in the middle of nowhere, build a log cabin and live as naturally and freely as we wanted. And that was it. Straightforward and simple, just the way we like it.

August 1998

I put a 'closing down sale' on in the shop and word spread quickly. Some people were happy to hear we were leaving, others were not. They all told us we were really brave to do such a big thing, and how much planning it must have taken. But we didn't feel brave, and we didn't believe in planning. If we were going to do this, we had to do it our way or not at all.

November 1998

I gave up trying to finish my work and just booked a ticket for as soon as I could to anywhere north of the USA. We'd decided that Bridge would join me the following March, when her contract finished. I'd just put the phone down when a client came in and wanted me to design and print 2000 brochures for him. "I'd love to" I said, "but I'm emigrating to the Canadian wilderness the day after tomorrow and I still haven't packed."

The following day I threw a sleeping bag, a couple pairs of jeans, two clean shirts, a weeks supply of underwear, my toothbrush and some money into a rucksack. I spent my last night with Bridge in the pub saying goodbye to the village, and the next day found myself high above the Canadian prairies on a plane to Edmonton with "Leaving on a Jetplane" going round and round in my thumping head.

December 1998

I stayed in Edmonton with Bridge's sister Pam and her husband Glenn, a true Canadian redneck who welcomed me into his house with open arms. I was to live with them for the next few months while I prepared for our big adventure. Bridge and I were going to go into the Northern

Canadian wilderness to pit our wits against the harsh winters, Mother Nature and grizzly bears, but first we had to find the right area, and get some gear. I bought detailed maps in Edmonton's Map World and spent weeks studying them in detail, trying to decide whether to dog sleigh through the North West Territories, canoe up the West Coast of BC or hike through the bush in the Yukon.

When I started to tell people about our plans to go into the wilderness they just laughed, and without Bridget to back me up I started to lose confidence. Bridge and I can take on the world and win, as long as we're united, but at this point I was alone. "What are you going to live on?" people cried. "There's no work up north! What happens if you're ill? People die up there regularly!" "You don't know our winters!" "Things eat you in the woods!" "There's no toilet paper you know!" "You're too old to do this sort of thing." But a stubborn voice deep in my soul would swell and give me strength like nothing anybody else can give you, a strength that can defeat logic. It rose from my heart and yelled Bollocks! Bollocks! Bollocks! and from then on I decided to keep our aspirations to myself, at least until I had an ally in Bridge.

Bridget and I are just ordinary people with no background in travelling, adventure or survival. We've been on the breadline most of our lives so we aren't scared of hardship or doing without, which was hard for these affluent Canadians to understand. We knew absolutely nothing about the wilderness, but in a way that was our greatest strength, because it meant we weren't going to underestimate it or let other people's fears put us off. We would probably fail daily and eventually have to give up, but true failing, for us, would have been to not even try.

January 1999

I was slowly building up a stock of camping equipment that covered the garage floor but what we really needed was a solid waterproof tent. I found a pioneer tent at Tent World which was heavy duty, warm and weather proof, but quite how I was going to set it up without the arm and a leg I would have to pay for it, I had no idea. I went to Canvas World instead and bought twenty yards of ten-ounce canvas, and a needle that looked more like a spear for killing buffalo in the rain forests of South America.

I had a rough tent design in my head and set about transforming the roll of canvas into the desired shape. It very quickly dawned on me why the tents were so expensive. As I tried to sew the pieces together by hand my spear pushed far more easily through the palm of my hand than through the canvas, and soon there was enough of my blood on the tent to attract all the bears in the Northwest Territories. I might as well have hung a sign on top saying 'Bear Food World - tight fisted pommies a speciality!' But I persevered and eventually had a tent-shaped canvas lying frozen on the garage floor. After rummaging through the woods for two days I had cut enough straight poles to erect my first Canadian home. I dragged the canvas and poles onto the front paddock and started to put up my masterpiece. Four hours later I was back at the drawing board and contemplating whether I could do without an arm and a leg.

February 1999

The next few weeks I spent collecting the final equipment for our adventure. I bought an old 1983 Nissan and nicknamed her Pricey, because she kept breaking down and costing a lot of money to repair. I also bought a canoe, finally finished my tent and decided to get a dog, one that would provide companionship in hard times, protect us from wild animals and help us pioneer our New World. At a rescue centre in Edmonton, Boris Lock stood out amongst Siberian Huskies, Rottweilers, Great Danes and hundreds of cross breeds. He looked at me through the cage as if to say, "Come on, Dorian, let's go party." I took him home and as he ran around peeing on everything in sight I proudly introduced him to Pam and Glenn. "What the hell is it?" Glenn asked, trying to sound calm but not succeeding. "It's a Basset Hound cross German Shepherd, his name is Mr. Boris Lock and he's my mate," I said. Finally we were ready.

March 1999

I spent the next few days washing and shaving, very nervous about meeting Bridge again after five months, even though we had spoken almost daily on the telephone. It's funny how you can be married but still feel apprehensive about a date, I felt sixteen again. When the day finally arrived to pick Bridge up from the airport, I was spraying my mouth with breath fresh, smelling strongly of "Brut" and had several clumps of blood-stained toilet paper stuck to my chin. When the arrival doors opened and the flow of passengers spewed into the terminal I watched nervously for Bridge. After what seemed like six planeloads of people she struggled through the doors under the weight of a huge rucksack and wearing a smile that said 'take me to the mountains'.

It was such a relief to see her at last. We were both shaking with nerves but after the initial clumsy hug we clicked back into place and strolled hand in hand confidently into Canada.

Now we were together, adventure called. After a teary goodbye at Pam and Glenns' we kicked Pricey into life, threw Boris in the back and headed west into the mountains. With the long straight road in front of us stretching as far as the eye could see, we really felt we were on an adventure. We weren't quite driving a Harley across the desert accompanied by an Eagles track, but we were driving, out of the confines of our civilised world. We'd left our watches behind, having exchanged them for sheaf knives Rambo would have been proud of, and I'd ceremoniously burnt my work suit and tie. I was dressed in old jeans, big rugged boots and a shirt that said 'Adventure West' in gold writing on the breast pocket. I'd not had a shave for three days for the first time in my life. All I needed now was a tan and the odd firm muscle. Bridge had her shades on, her long black hair flowing free, her arm out the window and her size five Doc Martins on the dash. Her baggy lumberjack shirt clashed with the upholstery but she didn't care, she looked happy but above all she looked free.

Within a couple of hours we could see the Rocky Mountains, where we'd decided to camp for a night. Their white tops glimmered like a pile of rough-cut diamonds on a satin cloth. As we climbed into their shadows, sleet began to fall from the contorted clouds. A dull lonely feeling crept over us as the windscreen wipers worked hard to clear the sleet from our view of the wet road. There was no view, no warmth, and our space had shrunk to the size of Priceys' cab.

All the adventure books I'd read never said anything about feeling like this. Each of us pretended to look for a suitable campsite but we were really both thinking about the warmth and security of Bridget's Dad's house, five hours drive away on Vancouver Island. Great! Our first night and we were already failing ourselves. Eventually we both admitted we were too scared to camp in the mountains at night. We weren't heroes, why should we have to be? No one was watching, so with relief we made a joint decision to drive through the night to the island, and 3.00 a.m. saw us pulling into the Vancouver ferry terminal. The night was illuminated by floodlights and the noise of huge diesel engines pumped out across the bay.

The sounds and lights felt like home, but we were embarrassed. We had been too scared of the mountains to make camp and enjoy their natural beauty. Instead, we waited in the truck for 5 hours in the noise and bustle of the ferry port, that had no beauty and was considerably more dangerous that a good camp in the mountains. As we climbed into our sleeping bags and reclined our seats we laughed with each other about the first night of our adventure. The ferry terminal car park wasn't exactly the untamed Canadian wilderness we had dreamed about in Polperro.

When we arrived the island was in the middle of spring, and quite a contrast from the winter-worn landscape of the Alberta prairie. Blossom petals floated with the bees on the warm wind. The sweet scent of hundreds of flowers filled the air, and songbirds were scuttling through the undergrowth in search of insects to feed their broods.

Whilst staying with Bridget's father we were safe and

warm and fed, exactly the right circumstances to rouse the spirit of adventure. We decided to take the opportunity to try our canoe. "Which end is the front?" Bridge asked with a confused look creeping across her face. "How the hell should I know?" I said, after studying the two pointy ends. We slowly worked it out by getting in and pretending to paddle, then changing positions, until we were pretty certain we knew which was the front. Then very nervously we paddled out into the sun kissed sea.

We'd never been in a canoe before and the only knowledge we had we'd gleaned from the film Deliverance. The bottom of the sea gradually gave way to hundreds of feet of deep water, as we found that even the slightest movements caused the canoe to rock and roll like a drunk at the opera. After a couple of miles, we were doing pretty well, and the feeling of being so close to the water was magical. We watched eagles fly above us, seals bob out of the water next to us and otters play and roll in the shallows. We glided along the spruce-covered shores, only hearing the song of the paddles in the water and the lapping of the sea. Rocks covered in seaweed would well up out of the depth and then disappear back below as we glided over them. We were hooked! Canoeing was excellent.

The next morning we tried dog biscuits, praise and blaspheming to get Boris into the canoe with us until finally we just picked him up and dumped him in. It wasn't long before he was curled up on the floor snoozing.

Growing in confidence and singing the theme tune to 'Hawaii 5 O', we ventured a little further than we should have and rounded a rocky island straight into the path of a huge ferry. Panicking, we swung the canoe for shore and as the swell from the ferry began to catch us I'm sure I heard the ship intercom say, "And on the starboard bough you can see two stupid pommies and a mutt, in a very small canoe too close to a ferry."

April 1999

We were getting reports that the mysterious North was still in the grips of winter with many of the roads impassable, so in the comforts of Bridge's fathers' home, where whisky flowed freely and fuelled our dreams, we decided to go 'up island', as the locals say, at least until the mainland north was free of ice. We packed up Pricey, said our good-byes and headed north through valleys carpeted in elegant firtrees and mountain streams bouncing their way down the rocky slopes. This time there was no turning back. This was why I'd burnt my suit, this was why I had a sheaf knife hanging from my belt, this is what my shirt said - 'Adventure West'.

To find a camp, we turned off the highway onto the maze of logging tracks that wind their way through most of the inaccessible parts of British Columbia. Some roads turned out to be dead-ends, others were inaccessible, but eventually one opened out onto a marvelous lake. We sat in awe at the almost-turquoise lake that stretched before us, a perfect spot for an early evening canoe and a camp. This was it. This was how we'd pictured ourselves in the wilderness many months ago from our armchairs in Polperro.

As if a warning from the gods, a cold wind invaded the valley, whipping up the lake and pushing black clouds along the troubled sky. Moments later rain and sleet beat through the trees onto us. Boris ran for the truck as Bridge and I struggled with the tent, which was acting more like a kite. After we were soaking and our fingers totally numb we dived for the tent and huddled together, shocked at how quickly the weather could change. The tent was up but by no means properly. I felt like an officer in the Charge of the Light Brigade, pushing his troops into certain danger. I wished I'd bought a tent from Tent World and not been so arrogant. We were struggling and there was no real need for it.

Our spirits were low, it was getting dark and we needed a fire, so we split up to scour the damp woods for firewood. Pushing through the trees made us wetter but we persevered and found enough twigs to make a small smoke signal. Sometime later we were sitting down to a luke-warm meal and I voiced my concerns to Bridge. "I'm arrogant, I'm a know it all, why do you trust in what I say?" Bridge looked at me with big doey eyes as the rain rolled down her face. "I believe in you", she said. How can you compete with that? Here we were, huddled in dark woods miles from anywhere, cold and scared, having given up everything we'd spent 10 years working for. The rain was beating down and the wind was bitter, we had a small soggy meal of mashed potato and cheese to eat and even the dog had deserted us. Yet this tiny lady whom I'd known for 11 years and whose lovely, long black hair was now clinging like melted plastic to her head was beaming a smile that said I was Father Christmas.

Later the wind stopped punishing the valley and as quickly as it had gone, calm returned. In the twilight we went for a walk along the lakeshore with Boris. A chorus of frogs was in full song and the conversation of owls drifted across the lake. Feeling more relaxed, we sat by the water, talking about our ambitions and reality, a conversation we were to have many times around our campfires.

Before we knew it the night was thick and we could not

see more than ten yards ahead. Boris was in the bushes peeing on anything he could reach, until he suddenly started barking. Our thoughts switched to bears, to big mean bears and of all the horror stories and blood curdling attacks we had read about before our departure. We called Boris and he came running back looking a bit ruffled but otherwise all right. “Time to turn in”, I said to Bridge, trying to sound not the least bit nervous. She agreed in a similar manner and we walked up through the wood to our campsite. Boris growled at something behind us and again barked fiercely. Our pace quickened until we were running up through the woods to the camp like two scared children clambering up the stairs, each not wanting to be last, in case the monster from below caught them.

At camp, paranoia really took hold as I realised how vulnerable we were, miles from anywhere in the middle of bear country and sleeping in a tent covered in my blood. We loaded all the food in the truck and locked the doors, but panic began to set in. The stubble on my chin looked the part but I actually felt like I was back at school, waiting outside the head masters office after setting light to a classroom heater. I told myself to get a grip.

Bridge reluctantly joined Boris and I in marking out our territory, peeing on anything we could that was above ground level. This was easy for us boys but not for Bridge. Every time I’d yell “Change!” Boris and I would run eagerly with tongues hanging out to the next position, but Bridge would get tangled in her lacey Marks and Sparks underwear and fall flat in the mud, which was highly entertaining. Once we could pee no more we climbed into the tent and battened it down, like cowboys digging in for the inevitable attack by hostile Indians.

From inside the tent things got a lot worse. Every noise was amplified. A twig snapping sounded like a tree being pushed over. At one point I was convinced a bear was snorting just outside the tent until I realised the noise, above my beating heart, was in fact Boris Lock snoring contentedly at the bottom of our sleeping bag. I tried to sleep but between "What was that?" and "Did you hear something?" I found it rather difficult. Eventually Bridge, obviously worn out by the day, was competing with Boris for the snoring champion of the west. I looked at her face in the dull tent light. Her mouth was open and she was dribbling but it was beautiful to see, she felt safe. I, on the other hand, felt very inadequate as I lay there with my family sound asleep and completely trusting me. I was scared, and I'd hold my breath at every sound and pray for daylight and safety. Sometime during the night I drifted off to sleep but entered a world full of 40-foot bears on the rampage, dressed and looking exactly like the big boys at school who bullied people.

Then, I heard angels singing. That worried me, was I dead? I awoke and sat upright. To my relief the singing I could here was not angels but birds. The horrible contorted shadows on the tent wall faded into glorious daylight. We'd made it through the night. We arose sharply, washed, then cooked breakfast. With the sun rising and the coffee percolating on the crackling fire, we relaxed and finally enjoyed our first camp.

With our first night over we were a little ruffled but had learnt our biggest fear was bears. There was not a lot you could do about them really apart from buy a huge Recreational vehicle to camp in or keep an AK47 in your trousers. We were vulnerable in a tent, and heading north up Vancouver Island was leading us straight into the biggest black bear population in North America. It was becoming more evident on every logging road we drove. A bear bottom would disappear into the bush or trundle along in front of the truck. Wherever we stopped there were damaged trees that looked as if they were straight from Freddie Crougers' log pile, together with bear turds that had an alarming number of crushed bones sticking out of them.

The second afternoon we pitched the tent beneath a huge forest of old firtrees beside a perfect lake and went fishing in our canoe. We did not have a lot of food with us so the thought of fresh trout flame-grilled on an open fire was very appealing. Although I had little fishing experience, I felt like a professional as I cast our shiny, new tackle into the water with all the grace of a toddlers' first steps.

Three hours later we were back at camp and Bridge and I were not talking to each other. Apparently the fishing in this lake was awesome but the only thing I caught was a bad temper and all our shinny new tackle now lay at the bottom of the lake. I had struggled with tangled lines, snagging the bottom, hooking my leg, fingers, shoulder, nose and clothes while Bridge had tried hard to keep the canoe in a straight line and pull the hooks from her hair.

The night drifted across the lake as we sat by the fire boiling up the last of our Campbell's chicken noodle soup. Our world shrunk quickly to the small circle of light emanating from the flames. The cold caressed our backs and the fire warmed our fronts and once again anxiety was running rampant through our veins. The only noise was that of the huge fish catching flies on the lake with a splash that suggested Moby Dick. We felt very alone as we turned into our sleeping bags. Another long night of little sleep was inevitable. When we finally dozed the bears took the form of ugly, fat, giants, singing "Fee... Fy... Fo... Fum, I smell the blood of an English man."

We were up before the sun the next morning and feeling very low. Bridge was trying hard not to show how much she was hating things and I too tried a few bad jokes to pretend I was having fun. The daunting thought was that this was it. This was the way we had chosen to live and there was no end in the foreseeable future.

We tried fishing again, this time with worms as our bait. The lake was so quiet, the slightest sound the canoe made echoed and bounced round the mountaintops mockingly. How the hell we were going to kill fish was beyond me. We were having real trouble fighting guilt as we put the wriggling worms on the hooks.

That night we lit the fire but had nothing to cook. Boris was quickly getting down hearted too. He hung around us for a while, hoping food would be served shortly, but eventually trundled off into the bushes for the night. We thought about eating our worms, then our boots, then the dog, but when sleet began to fall from the black sky we gave up and retired to bed. We were very disappointed in ourselves. Here we were alone in the most beautiful place we had ever been and hating every minute.

In the morning we awoke to a terrific down pour driven hard by an icy wind. We had to get out of this place and fast, if only just to see somebody else. We ran around loading up Pricey while Boris hid in the cab. Our clothes became heavier as the rain soaked them on our backs. This is how naive we were. In our so-called planning we had not thought to go to Rain Gear World and buy waterproofs.

Desperate to get out, we did not bother with morning coffee, but with no food last night and nothing this morning we were weak. As we pulled out to leave I saw, through the rain, a bag we had missed. Bridge fought hard to stop the tears rolling down her face as we unpacked everything to repack with the missed bag. "Are we having fun yet?" she whispered.

The rain was playing havoc with the track. Pricey chugged through thick mud, over washed-out sections and around fallen trees. We put the heater on in the cab to try to dry our wet clothes but all the windows fogged up and we could see nothing. Forty miles later we hit tarmac and the relief was amazing, especially when we found a roadside petrol station and cafe with real people, and food. Photographs of grinning fishermen holding up fish bigger than themselves adorned the walls. Some photos even showed two and three-year-old children struggling to hold up huge fat fish that would have fed us for a month. I felt a complex coming on.

To get badly needed supplies we headed for Port McNeill, one of the major logging towns on Vancouver Island and a small harbour town of 3000 people. Boris was letting out some noxious fumes after his greasy bacon and eggs from the cafe that morning, so some proper dog food was a priority. We found the 'supermarket' and toured the four inch wide isles, halted only by a shopper coming the other way pushing a screaming child in a cart full of coke and cheerios.

Leaving behind the music floating on the air-conditioned air, we headed west on mud tracks through the appalling mess that the logging companies had created. We'd seen the huge, bald scars of clear cuts stretching thousands of acres on an otherwise tree-covered mountain on the way north, but up close it looked like a nuclear holocaust, packed with burnt stumps and the tangled debris of unwanted trees.

We reached Port Alice in the rain, a very small and neatly kept town on the shores of an inlet from the Pacific Ocean.

The road west was closed, so with the fog as low as our morale we went to the local logging office for some advice. "Are you guyth's camping?" asked a rather jazzy sort of chap whose nose suggested that he had, with reckless abandon, jumped head first into something with absolutely no give in it. "But of course," Bridge replied sternly. "Well", he continued, "this is here the coldestht damb spring in 20 yearsth. Them their bearsth are fresh out of hibernation and their ain't no food growing yet so they'sth real hungry!"

With our path to the west blocked, heavy rain in the east and hungry bears everywhere we drove to the ferry terminal at Nanaimo to catch a boat to the mainland. We had just spent a wet and relatively sleepless 14 days, 7 hours and 31 minutes huddled under the tent that was proving not the least bit waterproof. Boris was, I'm sure, making secret plans to escape back to the kennels and cursing the day I picked him up. Bridge was dying for a hot bath, threatening mutiny and desperately missing simple, everyday things like a table or a mirror. I was just too tired to care about much except a badly needed cup of coffee in a Styrofoam cup.

The ferry terminal was bright and clean. No one was around apart from a plump middle- aged woman behind the cafeteria counter who seemed to have a fetish for wiping the counters with wet rags. A ferry was not due for another 2 hours so we sat looking over the bay watching the rain through tinted glass. We were tired, irritable and introverted. Our learning curve over the last two weeks had been vertical and we just weren't enjoying ourselves. Everything was a struggle, from getting a drink of water to feeding the dog. We were in constant fear of our lives, whether it be bears, rabid squirrels or mad axe men, even though I'd bought a rifle from Bridget's father, who insisted that if I was going to take his daughter into the wilderness, I'd better look after her.

The hardest thing to deal with was not knowing the time and learning not to care about it. Every morning, on waking up, one of us would ask, "What time is it?" Every time we stopped for petrol we would ask the teller the time. We had no use for time what so ever. We ate when we were hungry and slept when we were tired. But, it was the last thing connecting us to a normal life and part of us craved it more than a pint of cold beer on a hot day. We were comforted by the fact that we knew the time and altered our day to be in step with the rest of the world.

The ferry was full of people in designer clothes wearing sunglasses and generally looking very chippa and cosmopolitan, in comparison we looked like Neanderthals back from a shopping spree at Oxfam. Our hands were ingrained in dirt, we smelt of wood smoke and were dressed in all the thickest, warmest clothes we had. The journey to the mainland was not long enough, and we were awoken from our only sound sleep in two weeks, by a man from the cover of a C&A catalogue putting a dollar into my empty Styrofoam cup, as all the passengers made their way to the exits. We had arrived at Horseshoe Bay on the mainland where we took the 'Sea to Sky Highway' north.

At camp that night by the side of a fast flowing river we proceeded to cook fish, breaking all the rules we could about survival in the bush: Bears, by some quirky sense of nature, like to go for leisurely strolls along the banks of swiftly flowing rivers. Bears love fish, and fish stinks. Even though we were only cooking a can of tuna, the smell was everywhere. Of course, we didn't know these life-changing facts till three months later after reading 'True Life Camping Tragedies' written by Ivor Unluckystreak. This particular night though, we were very lucky and had the best nights sleep we'd had in days.

We awoke to clear blue skies, a warming spring sun and a wonderful serenade by the local songbirds. We stripped our white, sun-starved bodies naked and went for a wash in the clear river. It was arrestingly cold, and we splashed about in knee-deep water with the sun on our skin and with the feeling we'd been searching for creeping into our hearts. It pushed away our anxieties and filled our souls with a taste of freedom. We were really free, for a moment, a minute, a memory. And even this smallest taste of freedom, was worth losing floodlit ferry terminals to feel.

We didn't get moving that day till late. The gurgling of the river, the water glistening in the sun, the fresh smell of pine trees steaming in the warmth of the morning and the mountains standing like gods in the distance were all too perfect. We spent several hours talking and laughing, wandering the riverbank and digging up worms for fish bait like carefree children. It was wonderful. Laughter had been conspicuous by its absence since we started our great life changing adventure and now it had returned like an old dear friend. We were actually enjoying this and were stimulated by the surroundings. So, I went fishing and ruined everything.

Once underway the Sea to Sky Highway took us to where it promised, literally. Up and up we climbed through the spruce-clad Squamish valley bathed in pristine sunlight and crowned with a clear blue sky. Eagles soared leisurely on thermals as we drove up the mountains to join them. We were on top of the world geographically and in our hearts. We could see miles and miles of mountains, trees, rivers and lakes untouched by man. It was like looking at a baby's fresh face, unblemished by time or trauma. It was the first time I had seen to the horizon with no sign of human activity or influence.

We struggled to keep our nerve on the descents, and Pricey's dodgy brakes added to the already scary combination of steep hairpin roads and ice. Still, everywhere we nodded, peered or poked the view was perfect as far as the eye could see. Fresh, cold mountain streams supplied drinking water that surpassed any you can buy in a bottle. Deciding on a campsite was like touring the finest hotels in Paris or New York, being picky about where we wanted to stay even though they were all as decadent as the last and totally free.

One night we decided on a spot next to a swiftly flowing brook and started the camp routine that was becoming second nature to us. One person would collect the wood, whilst the other started and nurtured the fire and unpacked the truck. Boris did his bit by charging about marking the territory. The fire quickly warmed us and the now familiar smell of wood smoke stimulated our hunger. We were low on food but because we were in such a gorgeous spot I was not allowed to destroy the mood by trying to fish. Instead, Bridge decided to have a go at making bannock, an Indian bread made from flour and water.

We got the camp cookbook out for instructions and stoked the fire nice and hot. Bridge rolled up her sleeves and began to mix the ingredients with all the flair and flamboyance of a French chef. We put the small scones into our cast iron Dutch Oven and into the heart of the fire, then crowded round and watched and waited with interest. Occasionally we lifted the lid for a peak. We tried to get on with other things but were quickly drawn back to the pot.

Half an hour later we were glad of the wind that had picked up to carry away the noxious black smoke coming from the pot, in which we discovered the strongest and hardest substance known to man. We could house the third world with the bricks Bridge was creating. Even Boris, who is usually a have-a-go sort of chap when it comes to food, could not be tricked into eating Bridges' bannock. After a lot of swearing, a little temper tantrum and a bannock-hurling competition we settled on the ever-reliable Campbell's chicken noodle soup.

We spent a couple of weeks hiking through the mountains and enjoying the solitude. Life was silent, slow and magical. Our camps were incredible picture book material, and the beauty washed away our fears and regrets. We felt a real part of something huge, something natural. We still had to work hard to get off the beaten track. Although we saw no one, we saw their traces - a coke can here, a Big Mac box there, quad tracks running over saplings, toilet paper in the bushes. It was disappointing to see such things in a world that shouts raw nature from every rocky outcrop, twisted pine and mountain stream.

We were like toddlers walking around in a new world where we had to learn the basics all over again. Where to get dry firewood and how much we would need for the whole night. How to spot a 'dead standing tree', which was the warmest and easiest wood to burn. We learnt that to avoid bears we needed to keep all the food 300 feet away from the sleeping area, to wash all dishes thoroughly and dump the water far away from camp. We even changed the clothes we cooked in before retiring to the tent, leaving them with the food. All of these were government-approved guidelines for not attracting Yogi and Boo-boo Bear to your camp, and they seemed to be working. Boris had only barked once at something heavy walking around the tent, but that quickly disappeared when we woke up screaming. We were learning how to chop wood, how to camp discretely, how to work with little or no light and how to use the natural shelter around us to protect camp a little more from the weather. Which incidentally we were learning how to read, although that's pretty easy in BC, it's going to rain.

As we came out of the mountains we dropped very sharply below the clouds and started to see humans again, though this time we were not as elated. We had enjoyed being alone in the vast expanse and romance of the mountains (although Boris was a bit of a gooseberry at times). This new land, the Central Interior of BC, was arid, with skimpy vegetation and sparsely placed trees. We stopped at a little town called Lillooet and went for a coffee, watching the busy town going about its business through the window of the restaurant.

Watching people working was hard to stomach. Not working still seemed wrong and irregular, as if we were doing something illegal or misguided. Everyday these people worked they were better off financially than they were the day before, while we were becoming less and less financially secure. Our friends and families had kept telling us how they would have loved to give up all their responsibilities and take off round the world, but that they needed to work. Even though we were spending a quarter of what we did per day when we were home, we knew that our savings wouldn't last forever and we would have to work sooner or later. But we still felt guilty not working now.

Still, we may have been unemployed and homeless, but for the first time in our lives we were truly responsible for ourselves. There were no back ups, contingency plans, government hand outs or help lines. There was nothing to help us if we got lost or had an accident in the mountains, because no one knew we were there. We weren't moving forward financially, but somehow we were developing our lives in more important ways. We just needed to start believing it.

May 1999

We headed North West to Fraser Lake, where we knew there was land for sale relatively cheaply. We were directed to a Forest Service camp site by the cashier of the local shop, who said the site was hardly ever used because it didn't have electricity and wouldn't fit an 'RV' - a huge, ugly caravan 400ft long with everything from a microwave to air conditioning inside. It sounded ideal, so an hour later we were there in the pouring rain looking over the lake.

We erected a canvas sheet between four trees so we could sit in the dry and listen to the rain on the lake. After a 'see how many marshmallows you can get in your mouth at once' competition (which Bridget won) and feeling sick, we set up camp in the rain, then lit a fire with firewood already cut and neatly stacked in the campground stockpile.

What a luxury that was. Not having to scour the woods for dead trees, fell them, cut them up (with a handsaw) and pack them back to camp. Ray Mears had taught us to live by fire. If we were tired and could get a fire going, our spirits would rise with the flames, especially if a hot drink was prepared on a tripod made from green wood. We learnt that even in the wettest weather a good fire was possible. We just needed to find the right wood.

Now when we walked through the woods we also noticed things we might need later, such as a dead tree for fire wood, some Sphagnum moss for the best toilet paper, a patch of nettles to make a morning brew, or a Silverweed plant for its roots to use as a vegetable with the evening meal. A basic way of thinking was creeping into our over pampered and de-sensitised minds, and it felt terrific.

Fraser Lake was fairly close to human inhabitants, so we saw nappies, coke cans and other rubbish floating in the lake. This appalled us, and was enough to stop us drinking the water and to put us off buying any land. You couldn't see any houses from the lake where we were but it was obvious in other ways, such as an orange tinge to the sky at night from town lights, or the sound of a truck driving up a road. These were signs we were not used to while camping and they made an impact on us. It was like enjoying a favourite film but knowing it would be interrupted by a commercial break any minute. Slowly, we were beginning to understand what we were looking for and why.

We stayed at Fraser lake for a couple of wet days, trying to fish, hiking in the surrounding valleys, canoeing on the lake, and practicing cooking bannock and other camp recipes because fish was definitely not on the menu. Then one day, which we can only assume was on a weekend, we were invaded by everybody in BC along with their kids, their bank manager and their long lost cousins. They came in a variety of motor homes and towing boats with loud engines on the back, which they insisted on filling with screaming kids and tearing around the lake at high speed. All the fire wood was used in seconds by fat men in baseball caps, who sat by fires of gigantic proportions, drinking cold beer, swearing at the kids and yelling at their wives who were shut inside the motor home cooking the evening meal. They didn't switch off their engines all night because they needed electricity and central heating. We got up early, banged and crashed about, shouted to each other, let Boris loose to do what he did best, revved the truck up for ten minutes and blew the horn continuously on the way out.

Wallowing in our wilderness snobbery we drove for miles into the bush looking for a campsite 'out of the way of commoners,' but we hit a sharp stone on the track and blew out a back tyre. Pricey lurched with a grunt and a hiss to one side and with a sinking feeling we came to a stop. We climbed out into the rain for a closer look. The tyre had a huge gash in it and absolutely no air. The word 'bollocks' echoed around the lonely, rain drenched hills in the twilight.

After 20 minutes we found the spare and like all good spares it was semi flat, bald and the wrong size. I attempted to jack Pricey up, but the jack pushed into the mud without even trying to lift the truck. I was covered in mud and soaking wet by the time Bridge had a fire going and a tarpaulin hung from the only spindly cover that was available.

We sat down cold and depressed, not daring to venture beyond the shelter of the tarpaulin, up to our ears in mud and watching the driving rain beat the spindly trees and form puddles the size of lakes all around us. The sky was so low we could touch it as we climbed into our wet, muddy sleeping bags. It must have been around 7.00 p.m. God please bring the morning.

Morning came eventually but the rain had not stopped. Bridge started a fire and the smell of coffee filtered through the air as I braced the jack with branches and lifted the truck. It's funny how things always seem better in the morning. Now we found the situation a challenge, not a disaster. Although everything was the same we were mentally stronger, and after a lot of winching and rather nifty maneuvering we got Pricey back to the main road where she could limp along at 25 miles an hour.

The next town was 124 miles away and it took all day to get there. We limped into the town of Stewart late in the evening, after passing though some lovely countryside that we couldn't see because of the torrential rain. It was almost dark and the only garage in town was closing. A nice young man very politely relieved us of a large wad of cash and said he would get his boss to put a new tyre on for us in the morning. That meant we had to spend a night in Stewart and our hearts sank. Not that there is anything wrong with Stewart. It is a lovely little fishing town surrounded by mountains and over looking an inlet from the Pacific Ocean, but after being in the bush for a length of time town life seems really bizarre. In the bush you are totally free to do as you please. There is no one to stop you, no one to judge you and no one to take money off you for parking.

We booked into The Stewart Hotel, left Boris in the truck and dived into the bath, then washed our clothes in it. Our room became almost as wet as it was outside as all the laundry drip-dried from every vertical surface, but we had running water, a soft bed and electric light. Oh yes, and a television, which we watched for three quarters of an hour then quickly switched it off, realising why Canadian book stores are so full of self help books.

In the morning we awoke to more rain and got soaked just running to the truck. We were really beginning to get tired of the damp and wet. Everything we owned was starting to rot. We picked up our tyre and retraced our steps along the still foggy, Bear River Pass. Moving north towards the Yukon, we noticed a remarkable change in the people and buildings. The people walked as if dragging something heavy and their faces were weather beaten with deep wrinkles, broken teeth and bronzed complexions. The buildings were shacks lying between rusting trucks with no wheels, and the signs pinned to petrol stations started advertising things like 'Diesel, worms' instead of 'Cold Cola'. Road signs with large bullet holes through the middle carried pictures of a silhouetted creature with antlers and the word 'crossing' printed underneath.

Three days later we saw the Yukon far off in the distance with the sun glistening on its mountains and tree covered hills. After weeks of constant rain we could not believe our eyes. This was the beginning of a passionate love affair. The gravel road stretched up and over hills in front of us leading us out of the rain, out of BC and into the sun of the true North.

June 1999

To celebrate our official arrival in the North, we drove to Watson Lake for a six pack of beer. It's a small town of 1500 people named after a chap from America who came north for the Gold rush in 1897 and ended up staying. The town didn't start bustling until 1941, when the Americans made an airport to fly in supplies for the construction of the Alaskan Highway, which runs south from Fairbanks, Alaska, all the way to Dawson Creek, BC. That evening we sat in the warming sun around our fire drinking cold beer, something we hadn't done since we started this crazy trip.

The Yukon wilderness was made famous by such writers as Jack London (whose books include Call of the Wild), Pierre Burton (a famous Canadian historian) and the poet Robert Service. We drove north on the Campbell highway, in reality nothing more than a gravel track. The land and vegetation are arid and scrubbier than in BC, because of the extreme weather conditions and poor quality soil, and logging is pretty much non-existent because the timber is not worth harvesting. There are consequently thousands upon thousands of square miles of pristine forests. Even better, only 33,000 people live in the Yukon, a territory approximately eight times the size of England, 23,000 of which live in Whitehorse, the capital city.

After travelling north for a couple of hours we saw a turning off to the 'North West Territories', or the NWT as it is more commonly known. The road said 'closed', but being the adventurous types we turned onto it anyway. We had to peer through the brush to see the road signs warning us of sharp bends, dips or large leggy animals crossing. After driving for 2 hours we came to a 'wash out', or more accurately, a large hole in the road. Boris said we could make it so I got out and guided from the other side of the hole as Bridge carefully drove Pricey down the slope and into the bottom. All was going well until the road gave way under Pricey's weight. That was the last time we'd listen to Boris.

"Lighten the load, throw something out you don't need," I shouted, and laughed as the driver's door opened and Boris was shoved out. With the truck in the hole and buried up to its axles in mud we had to jack it up and shovel rock under the tyres for fear of Pricey rolling over and being lost in the valley below. Once we had the truck levelled and standing on a firm base, we winched her out the other side.

This worked rather well, considering I'd only read about the procedure in an off-road magazine at a friend's house some years ago.

On our way again, we passed amazing canyons, lakes and rivers untouched by human hands. Moose drank the clear water in the lake shallows and a bear sat on the side of the road scratching his rump, looking quite embarrassed as we drove past from out of nowhere. We came to another wash out, this time with a river running though the middle of it. There was no way we were going to make it, even though Boris again said we could.

Without trying, we retraced our steps to a suitable looking campsite we had seen an hour or so back down the road. We camped the night by a lonely river with absolutely no fish in it. After eating Campbell's chicken noodle soup once again, we retired to our sleeping bags, now dry from the Yukon sun. Although we had been in the territory two days we had not yet seen it go completely dark. This was truly the land of the midnight sun.

The next day we made it back to the Campbell highway. Our petrol gauge was almost empty so we filled the tank with our Jerry cans, which only just got us to the next petrol station 248 miles away. The chap that filled our tank took some moving from his chair. He was watching Oprah Winphrey talking about pre-menstrual tension on a black and white television that flickered in the corner of his dingy office.

A couple of days later we found an amazing lake stretching into the horizon. We made camp then drifted in the canoe onto the clear water in the evening stillness. The only noise was our paddles dipping gently into the water.

We found it very calming, paddling around the spruce covered shores. A beaver watched us from a safe distance in the lake. We must have looked like we needed a Davie Crocket fur hat and could not be trusted because he suddenly dived away, slapping his tail on the water in warning. The beaver has been trapped for its fur for centuries and still is today. It was nearly trapped to extinction at the turn of the century until new conservation laws were brought in for its protection. The beaver population throughout Canada has made a steady recovery, but they're still a little paranoid.

Trout rose in silver rings on the water. There was not a leaf rustling. It was like being in the pages of the books that we used to study over and over again in England. Their high gloss photographs stimulated the imagination and stirred our wanderlust. They captured the beauty of places like this so well, but they couldn't capture the essence, this feeling of pure freedom.

The following morning we arose early. The sun was low in the sky and casting intricate shadows over the placid lake. We could feel its warmth on our faces as we sat with our feet in the cold water and sipped our morning coffee. I looked at Bridge's face. The sun was just beginning to lighten her left cheek and sparkle in her deep brown eyes. I had forgotten how pretty she is. The sheer pleasure of this moment radiated from her smile. It's moments like these that are so relevant and purposeful and mean so much about this adventure. This is why we gave up everything and this is why we were loving it.

In a moment of rash impulsiveness, we decided to take an overnight canoe trip to the end of the lake. We took a few basic provisions, loaded them into the canoe and drifted out into the water. It was so nice to leave Pricey for a while and get back into canoeing. We still had a lot to learn but drifting out onto the water and rhythmically paddling together in the sun seemed so natural. We didn't take much food with us. We were determined to catch a fish. We knew there were lots in here because we could see the tricky little devils in the clear water below us. When we caught one I was going to have my photo taken with me grinning and struggling to hold it aloft, just so I could pin it up at a local garage to annoy people like me for years to come.

I let out the fishing line gently behind the canoe, with no great hopes, then positioned the rod at my feet so I could watch it and the scenery and paddle all at the same time.

The shore was broken up into little hidden coves, rocky out-crops and back channels. All of which were fun to explore. We disturbed a moose in the shallows of one such back channel and it took off at speed through the water to the other side of the bank, before disappearing into the forest.

We were passing one of the many beaver lodges - huge piles of sticks, trees and logs all jumbled up against the bank - and trying hard to negotiate a path when suddenly the fishing rod bent double. "Damn! We've caught a log," I shouted, "Quick, slow down." Bridge back paddled as I grabbed the rod. It was stuck firm onto something and wasn't budging. It was our very last lure and we couldn't afford to lose it, especially this early in the trip. Suddenly the line went slack. "We're free or we've broken it," I said, but the rod jumped out of my hands and I struggled to keep a hold as the line ran out at speed through the water at right angles to the boat. "It's a fish!," I yelled in disbelief, "I've got a fish!" "Yeah, Yeah," said Bridge but then a huge splash erupted 5 feet out in the otherwise still water. It was a northern pike leaping into the air trying to dislodge my spinner from its mouth. I was all fingers and thumbs while Bridge screamed encouragement and threats of castration if I lost it.

"My god I've got a fish!" I shouted deliriously over and over again as I tried to reel it in, the canoe leaning precariously to one side. Every now and again the fish twisted and shock waves came up the line, down the rod and rippled through my body. It was several minutes before I could start reeling the fish in. Everything went slack and I wound in fast. "It's still there!" I yelled, catching sight of it near the surface. The fish was tired and drifting in the water. But in a split second the rod bent almost in two again as the pike made a last ditched attempt for freedom. It shot back under the bow of the canoe and the line caught Bridge under the nose. "Duck," I screamed, standing up and swiveling around holding the rod at arms length so the line didn't snag on the canoe. After what felt like 15 minutes the fish drifted along side the canoe. "It's huge! Look at its teeth," I whispered. I plucked up the courage, grasped the fish round the gills and pulled it out of the water into the bottom of the canoe. It was three-foot long, and thrashed about like a great white. Boris panicked and dived for cover, wobbling the canoe ferociously.

Although we had really wanted to catch a fish, we deep down thought the prospect unlikely and therefore had not actually prepared for this dramatic moment. Bridge managed to hold the terrified dog and the canoe had stopped rocking. I grabbed the paddle and with a touch of remorse banged the fish on the head. A startled expression came over the fish. This calmed things down somewhat and the three of us drifted for some time on the quiet lake in a state of total shock. Bridge was crying with silent tears which she later told me were tears of relief that our failed fishing trips were finally over.

We caught two more fish that day and then decided to stop. We had enough to feed Boris and us for a couple of days and we couldn't keep them fresh any longer than that. We definitely didn't want to waste any, although the adrenaline rush and the excitement of finally catching fish was quite addictive and spurred us on to keep trying even though we were new at killing things for dinner.

We camped on an island that night about 15 miles down the lake from Pricey but we still could not see the end of the lake. We chose the island because it was small and because we could only detect old signs of bear activity. We were being extra careful because we, our equipment and the canoe were covered in fish scales and smelling worse than Plymouth Harbour at low tide. The fish was cooked over a driftwood fire, the orange flickering flames reflected on the mirror surface of the lake

That night we heard our first call of the Loon, a black and white diving bird that inhabits the northern lakes. It was a gentle haunting wail that drifted low across the water and echoed dully in the hills behind. A magical moment that sent a shiver down our spines and will last with us forever. The Indians believe the call of the Loon is a message from the spirit world, from long lost ancestors. To hear its call you can understand why.

During the night a wind rustled the trees, and by the next morning it was hurtling down the lake from the direction we needed to go. It was going to be a rough trip back. We launched the canoe on the sheltered side of the island and gently paddled round the point. Immediately we were into the wind and going backwards. Bridge crouched low in the front of the canoe and dug deep with her paddle as the waves broke over the bow. I put power strokes in and tried hard to keep the bow straight into the wind and not let a gust grab the side and twirl us around like a piece of driftwood. We could not communicate, the wind was loud and stole our voices immediately. The force of the wind hitting our faces hampered our vision and our bodies were wet and tingling with the cold lake water.

With heads down and bodies braced we paddled as hard as we could, not daring to look at the shore for fear of it revealing our painfully slow progress. I saw Bridge tiring and fought to steer us into a sheltered bay. Behind the rocky out-crop the water was calm, sheltered by the trees taking a real beating as the wind roared through them. Bridge was exhausted and in tears of pain as she uncurled her legs from the bottom of the canoe. I looked back; we'd only come a short distance.

After resting we again ventured out into the wind. We really should not have been out there. Our skills were limited and we had never been on a lake in the wind before. We were scared but exhilarated - fighting back was the only way to keep going. As our arms and backs ached we put our heads down and paddled as fast and as hard as we could. Boris was a little perturbed but instinctively lay still. We did this for miles and for most of the day, with brief rests in between. In the full force of the wind we dared not stop paddling for a second. I watched Bridge's body bend with each forced stroke. Her hair was wet and being flung relentlessly around her face. I was worried about her stamina. She is a lot smaller than I am and I was beginning to falter. I tried to shout to her but she couldn't hear me.

I heard what I thought was singing. It was Bridge, digging deep for the energy to carry on. My heart went out to her as whisps of her song swept past me carried with the wind. Finally we could see Pricey on the bank in the distance. This gave us extra spirit and we worked harder and harder until eventually we were in the shelter of the bank. We staggered out of the canoe, exhausted but truly alive.

The next day we saw the mighty Yukon River, a wide line of water moving mountains, building islands and felling trees. This powerful river flows the length of the Yukon and through Alaska to drain into the Bering Sea. Its history is unrivalled in North America with stories of adventure, gold and pioneering. Many lives have been taken by it and many more will be as it travels molten-like through valleys and carves its way through mountain ranges. We had never seen a river so large and unstoppable. As we stood on a hillside watching its path through the valley we decided to challenge its power and canoe north to the mystical city of Dawson.

The times of making these decisions are almost the most exciting times, only rivaled by remembering adventures after they have been accomplished. You have to then do what you decide, of course, otherwise the excitement of that moment will diminish and the memory will tarnish.

By paddling the mighty Yukon River we would be following one of the gold rush routes of 1898, when 100,000 city dwellers from the south struggled north to Dawson. On their way they encountered starvation, impenetrable forests, 50 below weather, madness, murder, the Yukon rapids and some of the hardest untamed wilderness known to man. 40,000 of them made it to Dawson, a ramshackle town with a casino and bars and shops in the middle of miles and miles of wilderness. Dawson was the biggest city north of San Francisco and west of Winnipeg and yet had no way in or no way out except the untamed river.

As we stood on the hill-side, we developed another great Amos plan. We would drive south to Whitehorse, park Pricey, load the canoe with as much of our gear as we could, throw the dog in, push off from the bank and paddle north. But passing Lake Laberge (famous for the Robert Service poem of The Cremation of Sam McGee) on the way to Whitehorse we could see the lake was still covered in ice. People in town said the lake would be impassable for at least another week.

To wait it out, we drove west and found a deserted, lake-side camp where we stayed roughly a week. We couldn't be sure because sometimes we would see bright sunlight for 3-4 days continuously. We knew time was passing by watching the position of the sun. We knew it was evening only by the fish rising on the lake. We were well out of sync with the world and it felt great. We practiced packing the canoe and stowing our limited equipment as best we could. The canoe was so different with freight in it. She didn't turn as sharply, or respond to a paddle as easily. But after a couple of days we got it right and we worked out a way of tying everything down for our Yukon River trip.

At this camp we felt at home and really began to relax. I would fish and even manage to catch one or two. We would walk the banks and watch the woodland buffalo. Some days we would just sit around the fire and talk about nothing in particular. I'd catch myself watching Bridge and saw a genuine beauty in her at the strangest moments - in her expression and concentration while chopping firewood in the rain, or making a meal and not getting flustered even though she burnt her fingers over the unpredictable heat of the camp fire. Then there were the moments when the sun peeped over the white mountain tops and lit her face while she slept. One-time moments I was glad I was there to see.

It occurred to me that for the last five years of our

relationship we had only been together in body, nothing more. Both of us had been too busy working, little quality time was spent together and if it was, it was spent discussing problems we had to address or working around the house. This was not what it was about. Our adventure was showing us what was really true and possible for our relationship. We were being together, really being together. We weren't waiting for the other one to come home from work or to come to the table for a meal. We weren't sitting mindlessly together on the sofa watching television. We were here, in the Canadian wilderness, miles and miles from anybody, totally responsible for each other and doing everything together. The only thing that interrupted our fun and loving all-day conversations was the call of a loon or the flight of an eagle over top. Whatever it was it would be fleetingly worth it, and not a phone call from a double glazing firm or more bills arriving in the post.

Our life-changing adventure was finally beginning to take effect. We were beginning to shed our entrenched way of thinking, valuing and appreciating. Since we had left our comfortable world in Polperro our muscles had firmed, our hands had hardened and our skin had tanned, but the overwhelming difference was the sixth sense. A sense that tunes you into the other person subconsciously; being aware of their safety and their comfort. A comfort that doesn't cost a diamond ring to enforce, just a cup of hot tea, an acknowledging wink or a gentle reassuring touch.

When the lake had risen five to six inches we knew the snow was melting in the mountains and that the ice would probably be gone from Lake Laberge, so reluctantly, we left our lake.

On the way back we met a beat up 1970 Ford pick up truck

weaving down the muddy road towards us. An elderly man about 600 years old was at the wheel, his teeth seemingly left behind in a tough moose steak about the same time he bought his truck. One eye had gone on strike and the other was shaded by the peak of a tatty baseball cap that read, "I wish life was this dirty."

"Hello." we said, switching off Pricey.

"Wha?" he yelled back.

"Hello, have you got the time?"

"Wha? I can't hear you my trucks running, if I turn her off she'll never start again." He bellowed spraying saliva in a wide ark over the inside of his windscreen. He swore, then smeared it around with his sleeve.

We pointed to our wrists to enforce the point and he moved suddenly, as if he'd sat on a nail. He thrust a grimy hand into his jean pocket, pulled out a wristwatch with half a strap, put it on the end of his nose and winced at it.

"9.30", he shouted.

"A.M. or P.M.?" we asked.

He put it on his nose again. "P.M.", he confirmed, with a shake of his head. Then we asked him what day it was, something that we later learnt never works with Yukoners. His one eye shot off at a skyward angle, his tongue came out of the side of his mouth, and after a long pause he said he had no idea, but Monday was sometime last week. We left, trying to work out what we would do when we reached Whitehorse in the middle of the night which was in fact our lunch time.

After charging around Whitehorse for most of the following day, buying food supplies, waterproof jackets and other knick-knacks, we were ready for the river. Bridget tried to find somewhere to leave the truck for a month, as I struggled to pack the canoe without being noticed. We had to launch from the city centre because it was the only place in a 20 mile radius that we could get near the river, and I was drawing a crowd.

I tried hard to concentrate on my packing and to stop Boris biting a Frenchman who had an annoying habit of 'tutting' whenever I put something in the canoe. More and more people gathered around as if Boris and I were a freak show. One chap came out of the crowd and asked whether we were going all the way to Dawson in that, pointing to the canoe and all our luggage. When I confidently assured him that we were, he said we would never make it across Lake Laberge and if by some amazing stroke of luck we did, then there was not a turkeys' chance at Christmas that we would make it through Five Finger Rapids.

I posed with some Japanese tourists for photographs and was talking to every canoe expert north of Australia about how we were deliberately doing it wrong and how we deliberately did not have the right equipment when Bridge came running through the crowd. We jumped into the canoe, waved goodbye, found we were stuck in the mud, jumped out, pushed the canoe further into the river, and once again jumped in. People cheered and clicked their cameras as we waved with two fingers to all the experts and glided out, allowing the current to catch us and take us north.

Slowly the river took us with it, out of the bustle of Whitehorse and back into the Yukon wilderness. After our harassing departure it was therapeutic just to paddle quietly, listen to the Ravens talking on the banks and watch the magnificent scenery drift past. We had no charts or maps with us, so every bend was an adventure. We knew absolutely nothing about what lay ahead until we were past it. Maybe we should have bought maps and charts of the river but they were too expensive for our budget and we didn't want to be glued to a map for a month. We knew where we were, and that was in Heaven.

We quickly noticed the difference between canoeing on a river and canoeing on a lake. A current. A strong unforgiving force that most of the time was travelling at 10 miles an hour. It was like being on a 3-lane highway in the middle lane. We were just swept along at a speed governed by our surroundings and left powerless if we missed our exit. Stopping, turning and braking, we found, in total panic stricken waves of shock, needed completely different paddling techniques. The depth of water varied constantly. One minute we were in deep water, the next we were dragging on rocks.

That night we made several attempts to stop at picturesque campsites but over-shot the approaches. The canoe would hit the banks at speed, bounce off, spin around and drag us backwards through over hanging branches before we could regain control and steer back out into the river with new punky hair-dos. We finally got it right at a sand bar and set about our camp routine. After our meal we rolled out the sleeping bags and cuddled and dozed under the midnight sun, enjoying the way our bodies felt after paddling for several hours.

When we awoke the sun was behind us. We lit the fire and had a long relaxing breakfast. There's nothing better than bacon, eggs, sausage, beans, sliced mushrooms and fried bread, washed down with endless cups of tea made exactly how you like it. Unfortunately we didn't have any of that except the beans, and tea that was silty from the river water. However, the sun was shining, we were alone and happy on the mighty Yukon River and dying for a swim. We stripped naked and ran head long into the water. Seconds later we were back out shivering and checking each others extremities for bits that might have frozen and snapped off during the mad dash back to the bank. The water must have been several degrees below freezing. The temperature in the sun was probably 25-30°C. We were on an island of white sand, too hot to stand on in bare feet but the water was glacier-fed and dangerously cold.

The current was swift and the river narrow in our first stretch. Evidence of flooding was everywhere. Logs, rocks, twigs and whole trees were jammed and piled high along the banks. We watched in wonder as this new world drifted past. We paddled for about 10 hours that day and reached the Upper Laberge section of the river, which had several large sand islands and a width of 1.5 miles. We pulled into a bank and settled down for the night. It must have been about 2.00 a.m. because the sun was at its lowest and the sky was flaming above the rocky jaws of the lake. We had a cup of hot chocolate after our meal and watched the sky and its dazzling light show.

The early hours of the morning saw us paddling towards the rocky jaws of Lake Laberge, more than 30 miles long and with an average width of 2 miles. It runs directly north to south and is sided by steep cliffs, which makes a perfect wind tunnel. It is for this reason Lake Laberge is renowned and feared. The calmest of waters can in moments change to 6 foot swells. The steep slopping banks make it hard to find shelter and many people have perished trying to cross it.

The river was shallow and slower here and it took some negotiating to get across the sandbars built up at the beginning of the lake. As we neared the entrance, the river narrowed, cliffs rose up and the temperature dropped considerably. We were putting on jumpers when we hit a 'line' in the water, where the silty waters of the river stopped and the deep turquoise water of the lake began. Today the weather was perfect and the sun was getting hotter by the minute. We were suddenly in the middle of a large expanse of open water, and knowing the lake's reputation, steered for the relative safety of the shoreline. The conditions for crossing were perfect - no wind, no waves, only the sun high in the clear northern sky. We decided to go as far as we could while the weather held.

As we paddled we made up songs and sang them at the top of our voices. We laughed over nothing in particular and this time the mountains were not laughing at us but with us. The echo of our laughter, Bridgets' singing and my rugby songs echoed around the cliffs while we lost ourselves in each other. Bridge looked fabulous in the bow of the canoe. She insisted on wearing her little black dress everyday, apparently because it was practical. It looked like she was off to the disco until she stood up and revealed her size 5 Doc Martins.

The sun drifted with us, playing hide and seek between the mountains. We must have been paddling continuously for 8 hours when we decided to stop and have a meal. We found a little sheltered cove with a washed stone beach. A bull moose called in the forests behind, as Bridge cooked bannock and beans while I tried in vain to catch an annoying fish that insisted on swimming up and down the bank in full view.

We felt fighting fit after we'd eaten and the weather was too good to miss, so we doused the fire and launched back onto the lake. We knew if a wind blew up we might be stranded on the shores for a week and we didn't have enough chicken noodle soup for that.

We sang, laughed and talked about our families, our ambitions and our future. We didn't care anymore where we were going in life. We knew we were going on an adventure north and that's all that counted. A happiness had crept into our camp unnoticed, a happiness that we had forgotten was possible.

After about the 17th hour of paddling, fatigue began to hit. Bridge was finding it hard but she wasn't complaining. She stands barely 5 foot and weighs little more than a big bag of spuds but she still keeps up with me, whether we are digging the truck out or felling a tree with a hand saw. She has a real fighting spirit, and she constantly amazes me.

By about the 20th hour of paddling, she was pretty delirious with tiredness, so I turned us into shore early. She was quite loopy, running around in tears, unable to make a decision and flapping her arms. I had to grab hold of her, sit her down and put a sleeping bag around her while I lit a fire. Over a mug of steaming hot chocolate she began to relax, as she sipped and watched the flames of the fire with tired eyes. She curled up next to me in the sleeping bag and put her head on my chest. A thin dawn light hung over the lake that mirrored the purple clouds in the sky. "We did it" she whispered, as sleep began to take over. I took the cup of hot chocolate out of her blistered hand and she curled up tighter as I rested my back against a spruce tree. The fire was dying as my eyes closed on the lake.

We were awoken by the wind in the trees. I looked at the lake and saw white-capped waves fighting and bullying each other, egged on by a relentless wind. The lake was like a monster that had just woken up and was fiercely angry.

The canoe, half on shore, was being buffeted and scrapped along the rocks fighting her mooring line in a bid to escape. From our camp I could see that the Yukon River left the fateful lake about 2 miles away but it would be hard work to get there.

"Come on, we've done it before," Bridge said, rubbing my back as I stared over the lake. I felt a twinge in my stomach as I thought of our vulnerability. We were miles from anyone or anywhere, and if we capsized out here, who knows what might happen.

Moments later we were paddling out into the frothing lake and it was frightening. The wind was behind us and uncannily cold. Waves lifted us abruptly and dropped us unceremoniously, spilling over the back and into the canoe. I tried hard to keep us in the direction we needed to go but the canoe was filling with icy water, making her difficult to steer and keep upright as it sloshed from side to side. We could see the river entrance, a thin opening in the trees, but couldn't reach it. Gravel bars topped with rough frothing waves blocked our route. We back paddled, nervously glancing behind waiting for a big swell. One came as if from nowhere and we turned with it, hoping for a free ride over the bars. The wave lifted us clear and thrust us several feet, then ruthlessly dropped us onto the unforgiving rocks. The canoe creaked and bent as the jagged lake bottom forced up through her skin. With all her extra weight, I thought she was going to split open. We minced along the rocks, then a second swell picked us up like an autumn leaf and threw us forward on a cushion of water. We were in deep water again and close to the bank. Trembling, we scurried to the nearest shore and dragged our battered craft out of the water.

We fell back onto the sand in exhaustion and disbelief. We

were on a shore, but where? "I don't believe it," I shouted to Bridge, "Only we could lose the Yukon River." We trudged along the sand looking and finally saw a slight gap in the spruce further up. With our bearings back we launched the canoe in the sheltered shore waters of the lake and paddled back to the river.

Back on the river everything was sheltered and calm. We passed the wreck of 'The Casca', an old steamboat, her broken and split hull ribs exposed and weather-worn. Her spine lay bent and twisted half in the sand and half in the icy water. Parts of her old steam engine and stern wheel were scattered for miles down river. All movement had been stolen from her by the river.

The steamboats were some bright-sparks' innovation during the gold rush. They were used to get people and supplies up to Dawson. Their design enabled them to travel in shallow fast running water and carry large amounts of cargo. The down river journey from Whitehorse to Dawson was swift and took 2 days, while the reverse journey up river was hard and against the current and took four days. The Casca once bustled with life but now as we drifted past, no steam whistles piped, no people waved, no children laughed. Only the birds hidden in the tree noted our passing. The river was the only highway in the Yukon until a road was built connecting Dawson to the outside world around the 1950's. It was then that the steamboats and the river were finally abandoned as the major means of travel.

The river was so quiet after the roar of the lake and we drifted in silence, struck dumb by the beauty around us. The water was a blue that could not be invented by an artist. The river was narrow with hairpin bends surrounded by steep banks and thick, mysterious forests of spruce. Arctic grayling darted from deep pools along the bank. This stretch of river, immediately after Lake Laberge, is known as '30 Mile' because that is the distance from the lake to where the Teslin River, a major tributary, floods into the Yukon, changing the characteristics of the flow northward. We stopped for lunch on a majestic bend, cooked bannock and dozed in the pure, soothing sunlight while Boris followed a lone wolfs' track that decorated the sand with a meandering, lacy pattern.

In my slumber I thought how crazy it was that this river, this bank, this sand had been here forever and this was the first time we'd seen it. In fact this was the first time we had dared look for it; and yet, in a strange way, it was like drifting home. Things were different but they were oddly familiar, like the scent of the trees, the smell of the ground after a light shower of rain, even the sound of the water. Nature, who only now we were getting to know, had armed us with these senses so we should not be afraid. I realised how stupid we had been all these years to miss it. Perhaps if we had done something like this on a three-week holiday we wouldn't have needed to change our life so drastically? But then, instead of having to rush back to work we were rushing into the unknown. So maybe we did.

More than anything, this experience was giving me a perspective on life. Nothing made me more aware of this than thinking of Pete, a friend of ours. The trees, the smell, the sense of realness, the adventure, the call of the ducks, the splash of the grayling and the love Bridget and I felt for everything, are all something he would never feel. He never allowed himself to. He had busied himself trying to be successful and to fit into society. But he failed - and so hung himself from the rafters of his home. Nobody found him until the paper lady enquired about her bill. He was a happy go lucky chap, always ready for a debate and had a smile to brighten any room. He was intellectual and knowledgeable and it really angers me to think he would dare do such a thing. He had money troubles that wouldn't go away, which is apparently why he escaped. I really hope that is not true. Money troubles are the worst reason to kill yourself. Life is not a free meal and should not be thrown away when you've had enough or it's cold and a bit tough. It's worth fighting for and it can be what ever you want. That's the amazing thing. It can be whatever you want. I feel so sad about Pete. With a little help and a lot of fight he could have got out of his troubles and be lying here smelling the pines just like I was.

I awoke to grayling rising ten feet away in the water. All we were eating was Campbell's Chicken noodle soup and bannock, so fishing was the order of the day. I watched the grayling feeding and noticed they were eating little, black flies on the surface, so I decided to make a fly and catch dinner. Bridge heaved a sigh that said 'whatever', and went for a walk with Boris. I hunted the banks and found a couple of duck feathers floating in an eddy. I stole some thread from the sewing kit and a small hook from the depleted fishing box and set about inventing a whole new species of fly. My first three or four looked as if they had come out of Chernobyl and sank with a splash that put the fish off feeding in a ten-yard radius. I scaled it down, added a bit of tin foil and tried again. The first cast snagged a nice shiny, remarkably stupid 11-inch Arctic grayling. It was like winning the lottery. I cast twice more and each time caught a fish. We all had a fish for supper, cooked over the fire, and they were delicious.

That night we camped at an old wood camp, one of several places along the river that steamboats had stopped to take on wood for fuel. The woodcutters' cabin was still standing and his old horse drawn cart was where he'd left it 60 years earlier. The stove had a mouse nest in it but would work if need be. Walking through the woods we could see where the woodcutter had harvested the trees. New trees were growing slowly; nature was reclaiming the land in her own time.

We stayed at this camp for a couple nights, fed well by the 'provider', my nickname for the homemade fly. Although we loved the fresh fish we always worried it would attract bears. We tried to eat far away from camp and leave no trace of fish anywhere. Even so, the morning we left, bear tracks were all around the canoe 50 feet from where we slept under the stars. And Boris Lock, our super-sonic bear dog, hadn't barked once at night.

The longer we were on the river, the better our canoeing technique and the more we learnt to read the water. We could tell a shallow patch by the rippling water over rocks, we could tell a slow eddy and we knew which side to take a bend so that the current carried us best. Our ears were constantly tuned to the noise of rough water, which we could hear long before we saw it, so we could brace ourselves for an often short but bumpy ride.

Having no map really made the journey exciting and the anticipation of what the river had in store for us in the next 450 miles was a topic of nervous conversation around our campfires. Our only real concern was the Five Finger rapids. We had heard so many horror stories of people drowning or getting stranded there, and we'd never been over a rapid in our lives.

We traveled silently through mile after mile of pristine wilderness. It was like entering the Lost World and finding a perfect paradise. Generally, Boris was really good in the canoe. He would lie quietly in the sun curled up amongst the equipment. The trouble came when we stopped to camp. After long periods of inactivity he was raring to go and would take off into the woods barking at anything that moved, then return to camp and pooh right where we wanted to sit.

We rested at another old riverboat supply stop called Hootalinqua. It had long since been abandoned but there were still 4 or 5 log cabins standing. One had a pair of moose antlers above the door, another had some rusting cast iron cooking utensils hanging in the rotting porch. The river widened here and became silty as the Teslin River charged down the mountains to mix with the Yukon.

We managed to catch three more fish and moved on towards Battleship Island where we stopped to eat them. Battleship Island is just downstream from where the two rivers clash and is named after an old steamboat sitting in the middle of it, where it was left for the winter many years ago. It's now surrounded by trees but you can still see its huge chimney towering above them, looking alien on the otherwise unblemished skyline.

The river was becoming wider all the time and the silt it carried sounded like sandpaper rubbing on the hull of the canoe. The murky water made it difficult to see hazards and further down we nearly hit the submerged hull of another wrecked steamboat the 'Klondike 1', which sank in 1936. Its eerie silent form just broke the surface as we drifted past, changing course to avoid its stern.

We had trouble finding somewhere to camp that night. Bear pooh was everywhere and the mosquitoes were bad. We looked at several places but one or both of us got a bad feeling about them so we moved on. It was important to find a campsite we were comfortable in, both mentally and physically. We looked for places close enough to the waters edge but high enough to avoid flash floods. We avoided long grass because of mosquitoes and we preferred a wooded area so we had some protection from the sun while we slept. It's amazing how comforting having the gun was but it always seemed strange to take a rifle to bed. I was more scared about shooting myself than a bear.

On some wide meandering stretches of the water it was possible to see the slant of the river as it flowed through this magnificent land, sometimes even up a slight incline. The river dragged with it whole trees with their roots still clinging to rock and soil. Sometimes they would be sailing on top of the water, their root span as wide as the sails of a Spanish galleon on the high seas. Other times all that could be seen was a twig occasionally bobbing out of the water. These were the dangerous ones nicknamed 'dead men' by years of river travellers - this tranquil river was a major part of the biggest gold rush in history, when in the summer of 1898, 7000 handmade crafts carried 30,000 men to Dawson in their search for the 'Yukon's gold'.

For many of these ordinary men the adventure and the challenges they went through to get to Dawson was their real gold. They had dragged themselves out of the depression and the gloom of their lives to face the unknown Yukon wilderness. Most took over a year to reach Dawson and when they did, they just sat around, then returned home a few weeks later without even trying for gold. They had done what they set out to do, the gold, it is said, was just an excuse.

We felt we had something in common with those gold seekers as we negotiated the river to the 'Golden City'. Would we find what we were looking for, or would we return home empty handed to our ordinary, everyday lives?

We had not had rain for days so when it came it was a bit of a shock. Thunder was bouncing around the mountains and lightening was forking into the forests when we found a tiny log cabin set back in the trees on the bank. It had no door and no window but the sod roof was still good and the earth floor dry. It was like a gift from the old timers.

The cabin was probably built by an unlucky chap en route to Dawson to pick up gold nuggets with trained gophers - ground squirrels sold to the gullible to help them dig for gold. In 1898 the word 'gold' filled ordinary men with hysteria, and all because a group of Yukon miners arrived at San Francisco harbour with wooden whisky crates, mud stained sacks and old leather suitcases bulging with gold. The word got out, the press exaggerated the story and over a hundred thousand men headed to a mystical Promised Land, the Yukon, to follow a dream. They were ordinary sane men who made rather inventive plans to fly over mountains in balloons, ride bicycles, cows, horses, dogs, buffalo, even reindeer though the wilderness in an attempt to get to Dawson and the Klondike gold fields. They bought useless equipment with them including folding boats, mechanical gold pans, x-ray machines and trained gophers.

We dragged the canoe high up the bank as the rain bucketed down. We lit a fire in the doorway of the cabin and cooked our beans while we watched the lightening fragment the sky. The storm lasted a couple of hours before a warm calm returned to the river. The earth smelt damp and the trees dripped quietly as we drifted off to sleep, listening to wolves calling from deep in the forest.

The next day we stopped at Big Salmon, another deserted settlement by a tributary. At one time it used to be a fish camp for the Northern Tutchone people, where family groups would come to catch and process the salmon that swam up the river. Graves filled a little cemetery in a glade of birch trees. The spirit houses standing over the graves were brightly painted and well maintained by relatives who have long since left the river but return regularly to be with their kin. It was at Big Salmon that the territory's first Commissioner James M. Walsh became stranded en route to Dawson and was forced to spend the winter. The Northern Tutchone people gave him a small log cabin but he still had little food, no long underwear and no brandy - quite a contrast from the decadence of Vancouver. He made it to his grand residence in Dawson the following spring, a lot greyer, paunchless and dying for a snifter, and made a ruling that any man entering the territory must carry three pounds of food per person per day plus equipment and tools. This became the famous 'ton of goods' that the stampeeders had to haul with them over the passes and down the rivers.

We continued down river, negotiating huge, wooded islands and fighting dramatic changes to the current. We found an old camp on one of the islands littered with rubbish, like a deep scratch in the paint on an ancient masterpiece - we were obviously near Carmacks, a small settlement on the banks of the river. After burning the rubbish we decided to head there for badly needed supplies.

Carmacks is named after George Carmack who had quite a handy knack of finding minerals. He started this community after he discovered coal in the surrounding hills. After a couple of years he got bored digging up black rocks, closed the mine and went north to look for yellow rocks in the Klondike. There, in 1896, he was one of the first four people to find 'Rivers of Gold' and spark the biggest ever sale in gophers. The settlement was later used as a stop for steamboats and now it's a truck stop; its population varies between 100 and 300 people, depending on what time the pub opens. We stayed the night in the campground by the river and contemplated running 'The Five Finger' rapids that were now only a days paddling away.

We were slipping away in the early hours of the morning, trying to leave the campsite without paying, when the rather diligent warden stopped us and charged us eight Canadian dollars. It was the best money I have ever spent, because of the warden's rather casual parting remarks - "Be careful in the rapids and remember to keep to the right." Being dyslexic I looked at Bridge who pointed automatically (after 11 years of having to) to the right. "Why the right?" I shouted after him. Without turning round he said "Because all the other channels will kill you."

We anxiously broke camp - the rapids could not be far away, probably around the next bend. We packed everything tightly into the canoe and roped it all down. If we rolled my granny knots would surely hold something in. We each had a survival pack, strapped to our waist, in case we got separated and couldn't find one another for a couple of days. We put on life jackets and climbed into the canoe.

At each bend the roar of the rapids got louder. Then louder. Intruding our space, stealing our quiet river, filling us with fear. Then we saw them - four huge rocky pillars standing across the river. We pulled over to the side. "I have no idea how to do this!" I said. "Stick right and hang on, I suppose," Bridge soothed, anxiously. "We should have a spray skirt, to keep the water out." But it was too late. We had to go through now - we couldn't paddle back against the current and Carmacks was a week's walk away. After a nervous pee we climbed back into the canoe and feeling incredibly small and humble, paddled towards the rapids.

My heart was in my mouth as we drifted closer to the grotesque rock towers. Ravens flew from the tops, laughing a coarse laugh as we went past the point of no return. We picked up speed and were suddenly in the rapids' trap, the pull of water too strong to escape. "Hang on!" I shouted. Bridge couldn't hear. We drifted faster and faster into the turmoil of frothing water. The jagged rocks closed in at speed, towering way above us as the river, 400 foot wide, narrowed to five, 20-feet-wide 'fingers' and dropped several feet carrying us uncontrollably with it. I fought the current and clung to the right. The canoe bucked and rolled. We ducked as the rocks seemed to lunge at us. The canoe tipped. I was thrown forward and lost control. I looked up. We were too far out in the channel, we should be on the right! I saw Bridge still paddling but staring into a wall of water high above her head. We ploughed into it. Bridge disappeared into the water, the canoe and I followed. We rose out of the water then dropped into a trough and then ploughed through another wave. We surfaced and Boris, drenched to the skin, was standing with front legs on the side ready to jump overboard, like a rat deserting a sinking ship. I could see another wall of water coming and yelled at him. He was making us lean dangerously to the left. We went down another trough and through another wave that filled the canoe with icy water. I looked for Boris. I couldn't see him as we hit yet another wave that engulfed us. Seconds later the roar was behind us and the waves were calmer. Bridge was soaked to the skin and laughing. "Where's Boris?," I shouted to Bridge. Then his bedraggled head looked up above our packs. He was wet, miserable and sitting in muddy water up to his neck, not daring to move and wondering what the hell he had done wrong. I looked the cleanest I had in weeks and Bridge's little black dress was soaked and clinging to her curves. We whooped and cheered as the current swept us on. We'd made it! The canoe was low in the water and we bailed frantically with coffee mugs, laughing like we had never laughed before. The tension, the rage, the noise, the fright was all gone, replaced by a quiet, calm and friendly river that we knew so well and had been travelling with for days.

Further down the river we made camp. We unpacked everything and dried the canoe in the sun. Our sleeping bags were hung up to dry along with our clothes. Some foods like flour and cereals were spoiled, but on the whole we had been lucky. We sat in silence drinking tea, watching the river and listening to the distant roar of the rapids, knowing that we didn't need to go over them again. In a strange way, I wished the rapids could have been twice as long and around every bend. But, I consoled myself with the fact that, with Bridge and I in control, we were bound to have more adrenaline-pumping, pee-inducing adventurous moments, probably within the next 24 hours. Only in yesterday's boxes (cars, houses, offices) did boredom rear its ugly head.

It's rather odd to think that this territory is only 100 years old because it is full of relics of a past life. We came across another cabin in which the roof had collapsed and the door was gone. Horse harnesses hung on rusty nails under the log porch. In the nearby trees a horse's skull bleached stark white lay on the ground. The bullet hole between the eyes was a haunting reminder of how hard the life was and still is up here.

One morning a lone canoeist came down the river as we fished for grayling. We were surprised to see anybody but invited him in for coffee. His name was Hans, and he'd come all the way from Germany. He told us in English taken from a Monty Python sketch that he canoed the Yukon all the way to the Bering Sea most years. We chatted for a while about the river, how he canoed over the rapids and if he'd got wet in the latest storm, then for some strange reason we asked him the time. It was 12.03 a.m. We regretted asking him immediately. Knowing the time was suddenly a real intrusion into our life. We felt silly cooking breakfast in the middle of the night.

Hans was fresh out of the military and wore a tatty moustache that hid slightly bucked teeth. He looked the sort of strapping young fellow that says things like: "With all due respect Colonel Sir! I think I should press the red button Now!" but obviously with a few zzz's instead of th's. He has broad shoulders, muscular arms and his hair was like every other person's in the military - very short and deserting fast with every shower he took. He had a nice boat, a kayak, which was fitted with solar panels powering a GPS, depth finder and fish finder and it had rather a fetching bullet hole in the bow just below the water line. Apparently he'd had his gun out and it went off, just missing his foot and piercing his boat. Consequently he had a bad back from having to paddle slightly lopsided to keep the hole above the waterline until he could reach Dawson.

He may be a little careless with a projectile but at least he had all the latest gadgets and gismos, from collapsible water containers to a Swiss army knife with a Black Forest Cookoo Clock on it. He loved flaunting them to us, and laughed at our grill over the fire, our blackened, cast iron frying pan, our battered canoe and our lack of a tent. He cooked his meal on a lightweight stove, that looked more like a miniature folding satellite, and in pots made from the latest lightweight metal used in toilet bowls on the Space Shuttle.

We were staying in this camp for a couple of days so Hans joined us and put his super efficient, easy up, fart deodorizing, bomb proof, mossie repelling, unsinkable tent behind us. He said he could never be bothered to light a fire when he camped and that he thought them a waste of time when you can carry a compact little stove to cook on. He was definitely missing the point of the fire but he came and sat around ours whenever it was going. He stayed in his tent zipped up and shut away for the whole of the following day and we didn't see him until we lit the evening fire and the smell of fresh grayling frying filled the camp.

He loved the fish but was jittery about bears, so he fetched from his tent the biggest, meanest gun I have seen outside a Chuck Norris film and talked to it as if it was a voluptuous girlfriend that thought he was hung like a bull elephant.

To demonstrate his gun he shot at a tree on the other side of the river a couple of times before it fell over. The noise was deafening and rolled round and around the valley as if looking for a way out. I didn't show him my peashooter, it wouldn't have gone down well.

That night he talked to us about the Second World War. He was only 31 but he had a real chip on his shoulder about how he was made to feel responsible. He talked about the 'good old days' of the S.S. This shook Bridge up, and she sparked up a debate about the death penalty while he cleaned his rifle. He got quite aggressive and with the kind of smile you see a Mutant Ninja Turtle wearing said, "And what's wrong with the death penalty? If someone stole something I cherished I would shoot them, cube them and serve them up in a Katopulpoofter." (which I've found out since is a potato pancake with lots of chewy gristle in it). I watched him lovingly stroke his rifle as he talked, then, trying to avoid a conflict, quickly changed the subject and nudged Bridge discreetly with my elbow. He made us more nervous than Boris going for a pee in town. We couldn't help thinking that we were in the middle of nowhere with a madman, and he had a gun.

In the morning we packed up camp quickly and quietly, trying not to wake Hans and got onto the river early. We almost got away but Hans crawled out of the tent blurry-eyed and shouted for us to wait. Trying not to upset him in the slightest, I nervously told him we wanted to be alone and to enforce this I said it was our honeymoon. He looked at me for a second and a big smile straightened his moustache. Then he nudged me hard in the ribs, winked, clenched his fist and made some rude gestures with his forearm accompanied by a sort of growling noise in the back of his throat that sounded as if he had a lozenge stuck. I nodded and nudged him gently back, climbed into the canoe and not daring to look back paddled around the bend.

Alone! What a relief it was to be alone again. As we drifted north the terrain was slowly changing. Hills were becoming rounder and rolled along with the river in a gentler way than the jagged, forced mountains further south. This was because we were entering an older un-glaciated landscape that had not been carved out by billions of tons of ice. There was not enough water in most of the Yukon to sustain an ice age so it never bothered. For centuries it was the only un-iced land around, supporting woolly Mammoths and giant bears, stretching roughly from the Pelly River up through the

Yukon and Alaska to the Bering Sea. This was the route the first humans used to enter North America from Asia, which ruined the neighbourhood and devalued real estate.

We noticed a figure standing on a cliff overlooking the river. It was an Indian man. His posture was strong, his skin bronzed and his long black hair waved in the breeze. As we approached he shouted to us, asking us where we were going. We yelled "to the City of Gold!" He lifted both arms straight above his head with clenched fists and shouted, "God Speed!" I thought he actually said "good speed" and yelled back, "Yeah, it's not bad is it mate!" Bridge looked horrified and curled up in embarrassment as the Indian shrugged his shoulders and disappeared into the trees. One of my finer moments.

We camped that night at Fort Selkirk, an old abandoned trading post at the entrance to the Pelly River. It was well maintained by the local Indian band and most of the buildings were in good condition. The newspaper used to line the interior walls of the cabins were yellow and ripped but still readable, most dated 1898. A graveyard lay in the woods behind the village, dark and almost forgotten. Old wooden graves split with time and faded by the weather leant at different angles the only reminder of hopeful gold seekers killed in the gold rush and military personnel killed during the building of the Alaskan highway. One night at a camp, very hungry after a long day paddling, we opened a tin of the great Canadian tradition, Pork and Beans. We were quietly searching with genuine interest for the pork in the beans when we heard branches cracking and snapping in the trees to our left. We looked at each other motionless, mouths half full of beans. The branches were being broken by something that didn't bend, was rather heavy and very large. But you try and disturb an Englishman while he's eating his afternoon snack, even if it is a bit short of meat. I shrugged at Bridge a casual 'who gives a shit' sort of shrug, and continued in my search for pork. The branches snapped again, this time just above the bank that we were sitting below. I looked at Boris, who was asleep. I relaxed slightly, because dogs, even if they are low to the ground and very stupid, do have some senses that tell them danger is approaching, and usually it's more tuned than mine. More branches cracked, leaves rustled and we could hear something breathing. Whatever it was, it was getting close.

"Hello!" I shouted, spraying beans across the fire as the adrenaline pumped through my body. The noise stopped but no one answered. "Hello! Is anybody there?" I shouted again, trying to sound big and tough. Still no answer. I put my plate down and stood up for a better look. My body froze, my bum winced and the hair on the back of my neck stood upright as I looked into the big brown eyes of a black bear only feet away. The bear was watching us with interest and smelling the air. It was huge. I couldn't see past its shoulders, it just seemed to go on forever.

I motioned to Bridge to slowly get up and walk back to the canoe, while I tried to talk in a low, calm voice to the bear. I tried not to stare at the intruder but keep it in view. Bridge got up and froze too, grabbing my arm as if it were a crucifix and the bear was Dracula in an old black and white film. I kicked the dog, who just rolled over and went back to sleep. I'll shoot the bastard, I thought (not the bear, the dog). We started to back off and edge towards the canoe, talking softly to the bear as it stood there watching us. It didn't run away like all the guidebooks told us they do. Worse still, it didn't get on its hind legs, which meant it already knew what we were and was staying on all fours in case it wanted to charge. Boris, alerted to us leaving, finally woke up. With a yawn he rolled onto his stomach and looked at us as if to say "You're not trying to leave me are you?" The bear moved slightly and Boris turned and look straight at it. Immediately, instead of swinging into action, Boris's ears dropped, his head ducked and his whole body seemed to shrink slightly as he let out the most pathetic bark I have ever heard. It was as if he knew what he should do but didn't want to get noticed. He got to his feet and with his tail between his legs and belly dragging on the ground, crawled over to us, where he continued his whimpers of aggression from behind our legs. The bear seemed to be undecided about what to do next. It watched us backing off towards the canoe and made a turn as if to go back the way it had come but changed its mind and strolled over to our plates. This was our cue and we scrambled into the canoe. "Lets get out of here quick," I shouted, "before he realises there's no pork in the Pork and Beans." Once in the safety of the canoe Boris immediately picked up the volume and gave the bear a right talking to as we paddled out into the sanctuary of the river, leaving the bear to do the washing up.

We passed the Stewart River where a derelict Hudson Bay store stood on an island overlooking the river, a true sign of how important the river used to be for travel. Now abandoned, its sign faded and paint peeling, the shop was once an important trading post for trappers and miners, miles from any roads or civilization.

A few days later Bridge became tired and felt ill so we stopped on a small gravel bar. It wasn't a bad spot but I wouldn't have made it home like Bridge did. I turned around from admiring my granny knot holding the canoe in place and she was in a sleeping bag curled double. I'm no doctor but I know when my Sheila's a few corks short of a hat. There was no way Bridge could carry on paddling tonight.

I was told to put up shelter and urinate in a far off corner, which I dutifully did. After twiddling my thumbs in the rain for a bit, I rather daringly wandered back to camp. I found Bridge lying in the sleeping bag crumpled up with cramps and vomiting violently. Knowing it was going to be a mistake I said, "fancy an Aspirin?"

I lit a fire and cooked a meal, as the rain became heavy. Bridge was weak and shaking, her forehead was hot and beaded with sweat. She tried to eat but threw up within seconds. She was obviously unmovable but we really should not have been camping where we were. The river was rising and the rain was getting worse. I moved the canoe several times up the island during the course of the evening as the river silently floated her and stole our space.

We tried to get some sleep but Bridge vomited most of the time. I kept an eye on the water level as it crept relentlessly to where we lay. We needed more time for Bridge to become a little more stable before we moved. It was strange, the river was one minute our friend the next our enemy. It made me wonder who was the fickle one. The canoe began to float again and I pulled it up to where we lay, knowing it was the last time.

Half an hour later we had no choice but to go, and quickly. Bridge was still very ill and it was raining hard when I put her in the canoe and pushed off silently into the swollen river. "We won't go far," I whispered, "just to a safer camp." The trouble was it took hours to find a safe place to stop. I began to hate the rain, hate the river and hate the wilderness as Bridge dry-wretched over the side of the canoe in tears.

Where is the chemist? I wanted to say. Where is the doctor? I was almost in tears myself as I paddled alone down the dark, misty river in the rain, with the one I loved in desperate pain in front of me.

Out here I could do nothing for Bridge and I hated that. Back home in our old life I could whisk her off to the safety and cleanness of a hospital. It was a both humbling and confusing experience. I now longed for the comforts and the safety of civilization, but I disliked everything about them when things were fun and happy amongst the flowers in the wilderness. If I'd been brought up in this environment I probably could have dug a plant root out of the ground to cure Bridge but I wasn't and I couldn't which really frustrated me. It was possible to learn these things - it just takes a lifetime.

Finally I found a safe place out of the rain to camp. It wasn't quite a cabin, but the trees were thick and stopped most of the rain so the ground was dry. Bridge was exhausted when she climbed into a sleeping bag. She was worn out from dry-wretching and just lay quietly, only moving periodically to wretch into the sand. I really could do nothing except try and keep her morale up. I put on a dazzling display of hand shadows on the side of a tree against the firelight. I thought I did an excellent rabbit but it went unnoticed so I made a cup of tea and sat with Boris for a bit. Things must have been bad - no one sits with Boris.

Several hours later it was still Boris's turn to do shadows in the firelight (he'd been trying all night but it had taken me ages to guess the one of a dog). Bridge awoke and whispered, "Dawson can't be far away now, let's push on." Bridge could hardly stand but managed to stumble into the canoe and we drifted silently down the river once again.

We could not find Dawson so we found a camp where we would stay until Bridge was back to health.

Bridge slept most of the time in the camp. I wandered around the island, panned for gold, skimmed a few flat stones out across the river, each of which sank with one unceremonious plop, but mostly I waited. Whenever she awoke I tried to feed Bridge liquids. I knew liquids were important because years earlier Bridge had saintly and diligently done the same to me after I experimented with a chicken and a microwave.

Eventually Bridge could keep a little water down. Encouraged, I became rather creative and made a mixture of salt, sugar and oxo in warm water to try and get some salts back into her, but that had an immediate violent vomit-inducing effect. After another three or four of experiments, each with the same result, I succumbed to Bridges requests and stuck to giving her water. A couple of days later she was starting to eat solid food again and during the next couple of days she slowly recovered, but it seemed to take forever. I was going nuts. I dared not leave her and go for a walk, I dared not talk to her because I'm not the most sympathetic chap and would have only made matters worse by saying things like, "do you remember eating that?" I spent four days of just wandering around looking for flat stones that I could plop into the river and trying to teach Boris to say 'sausages'.

When Bridge was ready and feeling fit again we packed up camp and launched back onto the river. A couple of hours later we heard long drawn out canine wails. "Wolves," Bridge whispered, but it wasn't like the wolves we'd heard before. We rounded a bend and saw a couple of buildings in the trees covering the hill in front. "Dawson!" we shouted. The wailing was the town's huskies and other 'proper' dogs.

There it was, the City Of Gold, and we'd only been a couple of hours away all the time Bridge was ill. As the current took us nearer we could make out the church spire, then the Commissioner residences, then brightly painted shops. In our enthusiasm we didn't realise we were on the wrong side of the river and began to be swept past altogether. "Come on, paddle!", shouted Bridge as we came to our senses. In one long and final burst of paddling we fought the current and the surge of the Klondike River rushing into the Yukon River. Our arms were like jelly and our backs ached when the canoe grated in the shallows below Dawson City. We staggered out of the canoe and climbed up the bank. Before us were the bright buildings of the mystical city, behind us 500 miles of untamed wild river. We had arrived.

The church clock said 11.20 as we sat on the embankment separating Dawson from the Yukon River. The sun was shining high and the dirt streets were bustling. It was in fact 11.20 at night but we didn't care and neither did Dawson, judging by the amount of people who were walking their dogs, grocery shopping and generally doing everyday things. The midnight sun charged the air with a pure and natural energy that radiated through the streets of this northern, picture-postcard town. It was a charge that is only found north of the 60th parallel in the brilliant clear summer nights of this time of year.

We crossed Front Street and walked on wooden sidewalks. We'd never seen a town like Dawson before. Imagine your garden shed surrounded by masses of other sheds, in the middle of a ploughed field full of bushmen and the odd hippie who looks as if he's just woken up, in total shock to find Woodstock over. That's Dawson.

The buildings had big fancy square fronts to them and were

all brightly painted so they looked taller and larger than they really were, suggesting grand establishments where people hold their pinkies up when drinking tea. But, go through the grand front doors and you find they're shacks. Some log shacks, and some falling down log shacks.

The roads were dusty, pitted gravel tracks. Wooden sidewalks skirted all the buildings well above the surface of the road. We kept expecting to see Clint, leaning against a pillar, wearing a poncho, chewing on a slim cigar and fiddling with his weapon.

Evidently someone similar was in town because there had just been a 'Rootin Tootin Shootin, yesssserrrieee!' One of the gold dealers had upset a miner. I'm not sure what was said but it probably involved goats as things generally do in these situations. To get his revenge the miner shot at the gold dealer's truck while he was driving down the middle of Main Street. The Mounties were on the case, all two of them searching the streets for a mad, drunken gold miner with a gun. Unfortunately, as far as we could tell, they had rather a lot to chose from.

We went straight for the nearest bar and ordered a cold beer. A band was in full swing, playing the sort of music that gets Bridge jiggling and writhing all over the place. The whole pub was singing a completely different song to the band and dancing not unlike Bridge. It must be something in the water. We quickly got in the spirit of things and I even tapped my foot.

About 2 hours and several drinks later, things were going really well and we were doing that dance people do with their granny and other wrinkled relatives at 21st birthday parties, where you all get in a line holding the person in front of you by the hips and snake around the building kicking each leg out alternately. Unfortunately Bridge and I were the only ones doing it and we were politely asked to leave after I kicked some poor chap in the shin. Which was just as well, as Boris was guarding the canoe down by the river and he's about as good at that as I am at dancing.

We had enquired earlier about somewhere to camp and were told that there were some good spots across the river, so we continued our snaky dance out of the bar, joined in a chorus of "Hi Ho. Hi Ho. It's off to work we go" with some drunken miners and snaked our way through the streets back to the canoe kicking our legs and singing "choo choo, choo cha." It was amazing the feeling we already had in Dawson, amplified I suppose by the survivor's high of having been so long on the river.

When we got back to Boris he was not happy and we felt like naughty teenagers as he looked at us with a 'what time do you call this' stare. We managed to clamber into the canoe and paddle, rather stylishly by all accounts, across the river to the campsite where we rolled out of the canoe and into sleeping bags.

July 1999

We were learning quickly that a lot happens in Dawson, or 'Dodge' as the locals call it. Two days earlier a girl had been attacked by a bear in the campground we were staying at. The bear had attacked her in front of several other people and dragged her off into the bushes by the neck. There it ripped and pulled at her body like a dog pulling on a large bone. Minutes later it had eaten her buttocks and part of her thighs before on-lookers could beat it off with logs and stones.

This sparked a big bear hunt and every hill billy with a gun, thunderbust, club and slingshot was pressed into action to scour the woods and shoot the beast. With so many people in the woods all of the wildlife quickly escaped including a bear, which was seen swimming the river and heading for Dawson. A Mountie in full dress uniform (for the tourists) which included a red jacket, wide brim hat and girlie black trousers wasted no time and charged, on a black horse, over to the swimming bear and shot it dead with his pistol before it made it into town. Unfortunately, a post-mortem revealed it had no ones buttocks in its belly. The girl survived but with serious injuries. She was on holiday from university, where she was on a basketball scholarship. Dawson, a town of 2000 people, raised twenty thousand dollars in two nights to help pay for her medical expenses. What a town! The place is incredible. It is full of people that look as if they should be selling The Big Issue outside W.H. Smiths but instead they break trail, shoot grizzlies, chew tabacco, dig for gold, shit in the woods and that's only on Tuesdays. One couple, only two winters ago, went into the Tombstone Mountains on a dog sled. They got lost and only made it back several months later, having survived by eating their dogs and walking out.

We took the ferry into town the next day. The ferry runs 24 hours a day in the summer, joining Dawson to the Top of the World highway that runs to Alaska, about 40 miles west. In the winter the residents have to find their own way across because they beach the ferry to avoid the crushing ice. When we got to the town it was bathed in sunlight and the air was too hot to wear a shirt. We walked the dusty streets in silence as we soaked up everything around us.

Some buildings were leaning over badly, the ravens

sitting on their upper walls. Rusting steam engines, boilers, pulleys, buckets, draglines and other relics from the gold boom lay in piles on street corners on the outskirts of town. New elegant houses stood side by side with one room, sod-roofed log cabins. Moose antlers were hanging above most doors. Huskies on chains slept in the sun on top of their flat-roofed kennels. Four wheel drive trucks battered beyond recognition and plastered in mud-lined the streets. Crazy piano music waltzed through the streets, coming from the bars that opened at 9.00 a.m. and partied right though to 2.00 a.m. And on every street corner adventure beckoned because all around this crazy little town were hundreds and hundreds of miles of untamed wilderness, literally butting up to the town boundary.

We went for a drink at The Westminster Hotel, the whole building was leaning at a 30-degree angle to the right. We pushed the door open and entered an almost pitch black room. It took quite a while for our eyes to adjust to the gloom after the bright sunlight outside. We stumbled to the bar with arms stretched out in front, like Frankensteins' Monster, groping for obstacles in our path.

"Welcome to The Pit, I'm over here," the barmaid said, waving her arms above her head as if guiding in a Bowing 747, while I was busy trying to order a beer from a stuffed grizzly bear in the corner. We bought two bottles of beer and found a safe place to sit just in front of the band stand, which was all nicely set up for the night's entertainment. It must have been around three in the afternoon but already the place was filling up.

Most of the clientele had obviously been here a while. If you were watching them on television with the sound turned down you would think they were in the middle of an earthquake in San Francisco. They continually steadied themselves against nearby tables and passing females. Most people wore tattered, mud stained clothes, had long straggly beards and carried long knives in battered, leather sheaths strapped to their belts.

We tried to keep a low profile and talked to each other with our heads down. It was a little unnerving being in there, so when Bridge scooted off to the loo I avoided everyone's gaze and busied myself in reading a little fact book about Dawson and The Klondike Quest by Dawson's own Pierre Berton. The facts are really quite staggering. The average temperature in July is 16.7°C, it's -32.5°C in January, close to a 50 degree difference. The record high in July is 30°C, the record low in January -52°C. The population of Dawson is roughly 2000 people, but there doesn't seem to be 2000 people in the whole of the Yukon. In the entire territory, roughly eight times the size of England, there are only two hospitals. But the really amazing thing is the history. At one time, the Yukon was totally empty of white people and it was the First Nations people who wandered the land fishing and hunting undisturbed. One First Nations chap I met summed it all up in a few words. "Back in history, we paid no taxes and the women did all the work. We just hunted and fished all day and then, one day, the white man came and thought he could improve things!"

The First Nations people in the Dawson area are called the 'Trondek Gwichen', which means 'river people', although just over a hundred years ago, they were nomadic. They would come to near where Dawson is now and fish in the summer, but in the winter they would go into the mountains to hunt caribou. In the Yukon, they were never forced to live on reservations. Because of this, their relationship with white settlers doesn't seem antagonistic and both societies integrate.

It wasn't long before the lure of the North proved too much for the adventurous types down south. Gold seekers started drifting into the valleys, including one Joseph Ladue. Old Joe didn't like hard work too much and hadn't had much luck finding gold, but that was all right because he was a bit of a clever git. He noticed dozens of men were finding a little gold around the Klondike region, enough to attract other hopefuls into the area. He thought perhaps the real money was in supplying equipment to these miners, because sooner or later a big strike would be found. So he booted the First Nations people off their traditional seasonal gathering grounds and staked them as his own, at that time Indians were not legally allowed to own land. He then built a log cabin and a sawmill, which also doubled as a pub, and put up a sign saying Dawson City, named after a famous director of the Geological Survey of Canada, George Mercer Dawson. He then sat back and waited.

Five days later, on August the 16th 1896, four poor, frustrated chaps, one of which was that cunning fellow Carmack, discovered gold in abundance on the banks of Rabbit Creek. Word quickly spread throughout the Yukon and people flooded to the new Dawson. By January 1897 Joe had had five log cabins built and was seeing a large tent city grow. By spring, the population of this new town was 1400, including two women.

During all this time, news of the gold strike had not yet reached the outside world. It wasn't until some of the 2.5 million dollars that had been taken out of the creeks arrived in San Francisco and Seattle almost a year later that the world heard about the rivers of gold and Dawson, prompting the trade in gophers and the massive rush north. Old Joe was laughing all the way to the underside of his mattress. An average night in his bar cost around 50 dollars, a hot bath 2 dollars. By June 1897 he was selling town lots for 12,000 dollars each and log cabins for 200 dollars a square foot.

By that summer Dawson's population had increased to 3500 men, 2 women, a Jesuit missionary and a skinny dog. In June the first steamer supply ship on the river brought 100 more miners, with 100,000 more on their way, and by the spring of 1898 so many people had arrived in Dawson that poor old Joe had to up his prices. He now sold a lot in town for 40,000 dollars, a room in his hotels went for 200 dollars a month and a one-room log cabin for 400 dollars a month. By comparison in the same year a New York luxury 4 bed room apartment cost 120 dollars a month. An arrival of 25,000 more men in June brought the population up to about 16,000 in Dawson itself and 15,000 on the creeks surrounding the town, only two years after Joe had had his brain wave. Those poor women - and I hope the skinny dog ran for the hills.

Despite Dawson being the largest Canadian city west of Winnipeg and the largest western community north of San Francisco, it was a law abiding town in 1898. The Mounties kept a strong hold on the law, there was very little theft and not a single murder. But could they party. A few happy, carefree chaps toiling for gold consumed 545,000 litres of alcohol during 1898. The nerds in the Canadian government quickly realised that in the north people were rather partial to a few halves on a Sunday after church, and that the government was losing a good deal of revenue from liquor tax. The problem was the Yukon belonged to the NWT at the time and all taxes from Dawson went to the NWT's coffers.

Wanting the revenue for itself, the government put on a fairy outfit, stood on tiptoes and waved a magic wand. Poof!, problem solved. On June 13th 1898 the Yukon Territory was born, a brand new shiny territory subject to Federal Laws. To top it all, it had a swampy bit of ground with a few brothels, a lot of bars, muddy streets, a handful of log cabins and a back garden full of tents as its capital.

Dawson was the 'Paris of the North', packed with millionaires and a blossoming high society. Two years after the town was raised out of the swamps it had casinos, hotels, two newspapers, a telephone system, opera houses and even a few more women (the skinny dog having run for the hills).

All this grandeur did not last long. It is easy to stake a claim - you just scrape the bark off the trees at each corner of a 100 yard stretch of land and write your name on it - so most of the gold claims were staked within the first year and there was nowhere for the new prospectors to go. They hung around for a bit, bought a T-shirt and went back home. Two devastating fires then burnt the town to the ground, the first in the winter of 1898 and the second in April 1899. People became a bit testy with the fire department and started to leave in droves, either to go home or onto Alaska for yet another gold rush.

Dawson tried to rebuild itself but the people were gone. By 1902, despite the new Dawson being a far classier joint, more like Brighton than Bognor, the population was down to 1000. Two world wars almost closed the town down and stopped mining altogether. In 1952 the town was cruelly robbed of its 'capital' status, which was moved to Whitehorse, because there they drank more brown ale.

I took a sip of my beer and noticed a strange chap coming

towards me, leaning forty five degrees to the east with his legs several paces in front of him doing the 'Doris Day - Thundering stage routine'. He bounced off my chair and fell into the drum set behind me. Symbols crashed, guitars fell with a twang and drums banged and clomped as he tried to get up shouting "some asshole pushed me" at the top of his voice. The whole pub was looking at me as the bloke staggered to his feet shouting obscenities. The barmaid came over and banged a metal tray rather tunefully on his head. "Okay, Okay, I know, I'm barred again," he said with hands over his head as he made for the door, which he missed by three feet and hit the wall. It was the weekend, said the barmaid, and miners were in town.

Gold is still legal tender in Dawson and all the pubs have the day's gold price on the wall. Miners still come in from the creeks with pockets bulging. They sell their gold in town and head to the General Store to stock up on supplies. Unfortunately for them there are four pubs to get passed before the store. Some go for a quick drink that lasts three days then return to the mine to get the next weeks supply money out of the ground.

It's staggering but after 100 years the general consensus is that only 40 per cent of the Yukon's gold has been mined. In 1998 alone, over 79 million dollars of gold was retrieved from the creeks, the total mineral resources mined from the Yukon over 113 million, including silver, lead, zinc and copper. The amount goes up each year.

During 1897 gold was in abundance. People played golf with nuggets as balls. It was left lying around in buckets as if ready to throw on the compost heap. But gold was all that was abundant. One silly sod held up a restaurant at gunpoint in the hope of steeling some chocolate for his sweetheart called (and I'm not making this up) Nellie the pig.

Only a few owned the gold, of course. The Kings of Eldorado, they were the nouveau riche who had managed to stake their claims first. Now they had too much wealth and nowhere to spend it. Dawson became a desolate place in the winter of 1897. There was no food, no booze and no women. All the new millionaires in town could not spend their money until the spring when supplies arrived. Then they went mad. One chap bathed in red wine costing 20 dollars a bottle. Another paid for a dance with a girl by giving her the equivalent of her weight in gold. Another built a bar onto his dog sled. Another spent 4500 dollars on hay for the only cow in town.

Some were wiser with their millions and built opera houses and grand hotels, only to watch them burn in the fire of 1899 two years later. One chap watched his opera house burn and said, "What the hell! That's the way I made it, that's the way it's gone!" Many of those arriving in the stampede every week could not believe what they saw and just wandered around town watching the fun, the freedom and the adventure erupt from Dawson and its people. Which was exactly what we were doing.

Dawson is difficult to pin down. Mountains and forests surround the whole town, and there is a feeling of isolation, but also of raw human power. I think it comes from the people who have to deal with hardship most days, the weather, the river, the wilderness, and the remoteness. They are used to setbacks and take them in their stride. Like the chap that lost his hotel in the 1899 fire - within twelve hours he was back selling liquor out of a tent and on the road to another million. We met a lady in one of the bars with a terribly scarred face, having been attacked by a grizzly bear years earlier. It had left her disfigured, but from behind the scars her eyes shone bright as she talked about her job taking people on tours into grizzly country.

While we talked to her we couldn't help watching a couple in the corner of a bar. Each took it in turns to put a blackened big toe complete with nail into their shot of whisky and drink it. The toe went into their mouths and they grinned with it between their teeth. The Sour Toe Cocktail, we found out, is a must if you're new in town, a weird tradition which originated as a dare. One newcomer years back thought he was special and could drive a riverboat better than any man. The locals were getting sick of him and wanted a way to pull him down a peg or two. One of the local fellows had recently acquired a log cabin out in the bush and had found a toe in the corner. The previous owner had lost it through frostbite and pickled it in a jar of onions. The story goes that the locals bet this big head he couldn't put it in his drink and drink it. The chap couldn't without throwing up and since that day it's been done regularly for years. With different toes, because drunken idiots keep swallowing them.

The next couple of days we spent exploring the creeks of the gold fields. All the famous claims were still being mined a hundred years later. We talked to some miners who used heavy equipment to mine and collected a lot of gold. Others we talked to mined by hand with a pick and shovel. Their claims cost them 10 dollars a year rent. They built log cabins and dug for gold when they were a bit short of cash and wanted to go to town for half a lager and a packet of salt and vinegar crisps. They shot moose and caribou for their meat, grew their own vegetables and heated their cabin with wood cut from the bush. It sounded an ideal way to live. They weren't rich financially but they were rich in life.

This was it. This is what we were looking for. Adventure was everywhere and the normal confines of everyday life were replaced by the actual struggle of living, with the wilderness and everyday adventure. We felt a little confused. We had only covered a small part of Canada and had not expected to find what we were looking for so quickly. We knew nothing of what lay to the east, and it nagged at us as we explored the secret valleys of the Yukon.

August 1999

To rid ourselves of the nagging doubt we reluctantly packed up Pricey and headed east. A week later found us heading straight into a torrential rainstorm as we crossed the Yukon border and back into BC. Our hearts were heavy and our spirits far back in Dawson City. We said little to each other as the rain beat down on the windscreen but we knew we had to see the rest of this vast country before we could honestly say we had searched out our chosen land.

Our world was changing with every mile south on the Alaskan highway. The sound of mud tyres on tarmac droned on mile after mile; endless forest gave way to farmland and plastic shiny towns; the road signs warned not of a moose crossing but of a fast food restaurant up ahead. Our battered truck looked like an outcast alongside the 40,000-dollar trucks with CD players and cup holders. Identical houses squashed onto acre lots crawled out of towns and ate the real Canada with an enormous hunger.

We crossed the prairies and entered Ontario, the largest province in Canada. We tried to keep to the bush roads in the hope of finding wilderness but it proved difficult. Ontario has beautiful country but it seems to be infected. For a start, the fishing was different; all we caught were yards and yards of other people's fishing line and discarded tackle. At campsites, even the relatively remote ones, we had to put up with old beer cans, rubbish and human turds littering the bushes. RV's were all over the countryside like a bad rash. And all the best lakes were government-run campgrounds with shopping malls and amusement arcades, or they were surrounded by holiday homes that butt up to the waters edge.

The east of Canada has a hundred or so more years of history than the west and several hundred more than the north. Humans have had time to infiltrate the wilderness and change the beauty and the roughness to suit their means and to civilize their surroundings, which was very disappointing.

We knew Ontario had true wilderness but it was far off to the north and would take some finding. We would need a floatplane and several thousand American dollars to be able to access it, which seemed very bizarre after coming from the vast untouched wilderness of the Yukon.

We searched for land for sale knowing we would not like it. 160 acres for £4000 sterling was the cheapest price and we would have snapped it up, had we come out here first and not discovered the Yukon. But the land was not raw, and we could not do what we wanted with it. It was subject to an amazing amount of restrictions even far out in the so-called wilderness.

'Outside', which is what Yukoners call the rest of Canada, was putting a strange and depressing pressure on us. We didn't fit in. We had no designer clothes or fancy truck. There was no way we could keep up with our neighbours even if we had any and down here that's what you are expected to do. Morale was very low as we longed for the Yukon. We felt foolish and irresponsible chasing a dream when we were in our thirties. I kept thinking of my father's words - "Are you sure you know what you're doing. You have to think what you're putting Bridget through." I caught sight of myself in Priceys' rear view mirror and was stunned. I looked awful. I squinted and wrinkles exploded over my face as I glared back into my own eyes. I hated what I saw. A dreamer. A drifter, a man endlessly seeking and getting nowhere because he couldn't accept the benefits in front of him. We were homeless and short of money. We wore the same clothes most days and everything we owned we could fit into our worn out truck with easy room for a scout troop. When would we know we had failed? When would be the time to give in and go home...? Our so called adventure now felt wrong, very wrong.

At our Ontario campsites, we missed the beaver splashing its tail on the water, the quiet nights, the darkness of the rivers. It wasn't the bears we were afraid of out here, it was the humans. We had no tent, so it was hard to escape the prying eyes of the passers by. We did have some amazing camps, watching fireflies dancing in the bushes, listening to crickets sing all night and seeing ospreys dive for fish as we swam. But Ontario was just not for us. If you like to drive to a once beautiful lake, now surrounded by holiday homes, put a fast boat in the water and have fun speeding around, then Ontario may be right up your street. All we wanted to do was listen to the trout rise, watch the eagles and be haunted by the call of the loon. It was imperative to find this, because we knew it was there and we knew how real it was.

September 1999

One evening we drove miles and miles on a dirt road to a lake that looked perfect on the map. When we reached its shores we had no room to camp. It was completely taken by holiday homes with signs that read 'Private Property' or 'No Trespassing'. The next morning found us back on the main highway heading north, heading home, back to the Yukon. It would have been easy and affordable to buy land in Ontario, build a cabin and just experiment with the bush life but that was not what we wanted. We had chosen the hard route, started it, loved it and now intended to finish it. Suddenly we felt free again. Free of troubles, free of worries and glad to be on an adventure. The people in Edmonton had been right from bugs to bears, things do eat you in the bush and yes, there wasn't much toilet paper around. But we could live with being bitten and no toiletries. The people in Polperro had been very wrong - we were definitely not too old to try this and never will be. We felt eighteen and full of life as we charged north once again.

Before we had finished our rather tuneful "north to Alaska" chorus we were in Alberta. And we literally entered it with a bang. Something under the truck just couldn't stand looking at wheatfields any more and decided to end it all, nearly taking us with it. Pricey weaved across the road, like a chicken in two minds where to go, then made a few geometric crop circles in the roadside wheat before coming to an abrupt stop. We had snapped a front axle, which was now hanging limply after ploughing an elegant groove in the road for several yards behind us. Bridge paced up and down the windswept road in her little black dress whispering "bloody bollocks" over and over.

I sprung into action, unloaded the tool kit (an adjustable spanner and some hay wire) and wired the axle together. The front wheel sloped at an interesting angle but after a few test-drives, it seemed to be doing its job of going round and round. We again set off.

All was going to plan and several hundred, featureless kilometres passed before the transmission blew up with another spectacular bang. Pricey was having a mid-life crisis. She had decided life was too hard dragging a couple of lost limeys across the country and instead wanted to be a chicken house or something equally immobile. We were only a couple of hundred kilometres from Pam and Glenn's where we could again impose ourselves and get Pricey to counselling. We found a phone about an hours walk north on the highway and called in the cavalry. Several hours later Glenn arrived with a trailer, a big smile and a phrase I knew only too well about stupid Pommies.

As always, Pam and Glenn were pleased to see us and were the best of hosts, but we could not settle. We were supposed to be heading back to the Yukon and into adventure. However, Pricey had other ideas and had gone into retirement. We had little money left and the harsh Canadian winter was a month away. After a lot of agonizing, a lot of kicking Pricey, a lot of phoning garages for quotes and a lot of blaspheming, we made a really hard decision to stay where we were, work in Edmonton for the winter and return to the Yukon in the Spring.

What a disappointment. It was a really hard decision that pained us both. We should have been able to cope with this set back and carry on. If we were miles from anywhere we would have beaten the problems and continued on our way. But because we were so close to family our decision was flawed. We opted for the easy route and we knew it. Woefully, we unloaded our belongings and carried them to the barn.

We put the canoe on its side and rested the paddles and fishing rods inside. Next to that we stowed our sleeping bags, cast iron frying pans, tent, wood stove and mossie net then covered everything with a tarp. It was like laying to rest a loved one. Our adventure was over and we weren't ready. Pricey would live up to her name and would cost a fortune to fix so we pushed her into the back paddock for the chickens to live in. She stood in the long grass, alone but proud. She was our house cow, put out to pasture.

Everything seemed so final. We bought some newspapers and looked for jobs. We bought some new clothes to look presentable and hopefully put an end to people throwing pennies at us whenever we sat down. I even shaved the bird's nest off my face.

As the days passed we tried hard to fit into the confines of living a civilized life but with each day found it more and more difficult. After living exactly how we'd wanted, doing what we wanted, answering to nobody except ourselves and feeling like millionaires, we now felt like outsiders. We no longer fit into the nameless, faceless society that we found ourselves in, that insisted on stripping us of our individuality, categorizing us and numbering us. Of course we liked some of the benefits it had to offer, like health care, running water and toilet paper, but at what cost did they come? Within days of our decision to stay in Edmonton and work for the winter we felt society's shackles, tying us down. They forced us to fit in, to look a certain way and abide by countless laws we didn't know existed until we broke them. Time made us eat when we were not hungry, sleep when we were not tired and rush to wait in line. Even Boris was affected by society. The pressure was on to remove his testicles so he would act less like a dog and more like an ornament, to make him eat dried food and to tie him up because he got in the way.

We were no longer amongst endless trees, a timeless river or a still and forgotten lake. We were in a shiny, plastic, 'happy' financed world. Full of pressures to succeed, full of the pressures of failure. There were people all around us that nothing ever happened to. They were never really frightened, challenged, exhausted, exhilarated, hungry, depressed or set free. Few have seen an eagle catch a fish, or heard the true silence that comes with being totally alone. I can almost guarantee that very few have killed to satisfy a hunger that consumes and weakens them. People here are scared of the unknown, of their cholesterol levels, of global warming - but their biggest fear is each other, and that's because they live in a world that breeds violence and disrespect. That's the saddest thing of all.

We had passed the point of no return, the point where you can't and won't fit into the norm. The point where it was necessary to make our own life and no longer dream, and that scared us.

October 1999

One day Bridge had an interview for a waitress job with one of the many chain restaurants there are in North America. It was a job she could do standing on her head. She dressed up and looked a million dollars when she left the house. A few hours later she returned, a down trodden, depressed individual. She was apparently too old for the job. They didn't exactly say she was but it was made apparent in other ways. That was it! That was her last straw. After being confined in the house, wearing make up, listening to tampon adverts and trying to find a job for three weeks, Bridge decided enough was enough and jumped on a bus to the Yukon the next day. I, unfortunately, had just committed myself to being a labourer on the construction site of a sewage plant for the cowboy town Panoka, just south of Edmonton. Bridge left without me and a week later arrived in Dawson City, finding two jobs and accommodation on the same day. It was so easy in the 'real world'. The difference from Edmonton was astonishing. In Dawson they took you as you were.

Things had changed slightly. My wife is a stubborn old hag sometimes but this was really something else. I couldn't bear the thought of being stuck in Edmonton for the winter while Bridge was in the north. Before I left for my job, I booted the chickens out of Pricey, dragged her unceremoniously out of the back paddock and towed her to the nearest garage with instructions to 'fix her up good', as they say in this part of the world. Then I left for a month's work and helped build a sewer pit. Exciting stuff.

November 1999

A month later I couldn't wait to get going but I still didn't have enough money to pay Pricey's bill and to buy the petrol north. Reluctantly I worked for another couple of weeks, then told the boss he was a bully and promptly lost my job. Great. I hitchhiked out of the cowboy town back to Edmonton and to the garage where Pricey was waiting for me. She had new shiny bits of metal bolted to the rusty old bits. Chicken poop was still on the seats and the Yukon mud was still in the tyres. Apart from the new shiny bits she looked exactly the same and definitely not $2000 better off.

The red wood stain of the barn was glowing in the afternoon sun and the knee-high grass waved like a sea around its base when I rolled up to collect our equipment. I swung open the heavy wooden doors and the rusty iron hinges creaked with their weight until the doors jammed in century old grooves worn into the dirt. Pigeons flew on clapping wings from the rafters and out through a broken window at the far end. The blue tarp covering our belongings was now coated in a layer of dust and an artistic array of pigeon poop. The musty smell of old straw filled the barn and the quiet swishing of a horse tail was the only sound I heard as I pulled back the tarp. Our adventure was back on.

I reloaded the truck with cast iron pans blackened by fire. With fishing rods with dried worms still encrusted on the hooks. With musty sleeping bags and tarps full of spark burns. I put the axe and paddles down one side of the truck, packed in the tent and the mossie nets. The water container still had water in it from one of the Ontario lakes - it was cold and still tasted fresh. Finally I crowned Pricey with the red canoe that stretched her length. I stood back and admired our old truck and tired equipment. It was all we had in our new life, but it was all we needed.

In the morning Boris and I were on the road north. The prairie was slowly giving way to vast areas of woodland. Towns were becoming smaller and farther apart as we drove for mile after mile. It has always puzzled why a country that covers nearly 4,000,000 square miles, is 45% forest and 8% fresh water lakes, has 80% of its population living so close together and within 200 miles from the US border.

Two days later we drove into the mountains and hit snow. Everywhere was quiet and still, each little cafe and roadhouse was boarded up for the winter and no one was around. The road had not been ploughed for some time and the hairpin bends took a lot of negotiating. I had just negotiated such a bend and was travelling down a rather steep hill, when out of nowhere a frolicking band of caribou decided to cross the road in front of me. I could do nothing except hit the brakes. Everybody knows you don't hit the brakes in snow. Well no, of course you don't, except if Rudolf and his chums haven't read the green cross code lately.

I went into the sort of spin Damon Hill did once. I was waiting for the inevitable caribou carcass to come and join me in the driving seat through the windscreen, when I came to a stop across the middle of the road. Snow had showered onto the windscreen and everything was dark inside the cab. Boris rolled over and signed a 'what now?' sigh, as I opened the door and got out of the truck. I was in trouble. Ice fog was thick in the air and I was lost. I hadn't gone off the road - although this would be a far better story if I had gone careering down a ravine with a caribou carcass and had to live on it until a tourist found me late in the spring, talking to squirrels and scratching my ear with my foot. No, I was simply lost. I couldn't determine which way I had been travelling.

I tried to retrace my rather elegant skid marks but lost them in the encrusted road surface made by other infrequent travellers. I could find where the caribou crossed, thanks to Boris charging off the road at right angles, barking profusely. He went to the right, which, knowing Boris meant the caribou were to the left and had crossed from the right. But I couldn't trust Boris not to go a completely different way. The only thing he ever caught was a blind mouse that haplessly blundered into him while he slept one night and even then I had to kill it for him with the frying pan. I walked up the road for perhaps a mile and finally worked out that most of the tracks in the road were heading south and the north side of the road was a little less trodden. Success! All I had to do now was wait for Boris to return from Alaska.

A week later the lights of Dawson City were visible and after 6 days of continuous driving I crossed the Klondike River into the town, shrouded in ice fog from the Yukon River. Dawson was dark and covered in snow, the temperature was -25°C and no one was around.

Snow banks were piled high on every street corner. Road signs were covered with sparkling blankets of frost and ice. A dog team lay curled up in the snow on the half-frozen river, their faces tucked under their tails, their packed sled decorated with snow powder from the trail. A canoe was pulled onto the ice at the edge of the open water. It had no snow on it and a trail of footprints wound their way through the deep snow to shore. This was the last town north on the Klondike highway and it was apparent in every howling dog, dark street and frosted window. The contrast from the Dawson we saw in the summer was horrifying.

I parked Pricey outside the local hotel. The place looked shut but ragtime piano music jived out across the quiet streets from behind the closed door and heavily curtained windows. I coaxed Boris out of the truck. He was desperate for a pee but only stood shivering next to me, looking around and wondering where the hell I had brought him. The night air was working its way into my bones minutes after I stepped into it and I was just wondering what I was doing here in the dead of winter when two Indians walked up laughing.

"Is that your dog," one said, cocking his head in Boris's direction. Before I could answer the other one chipped into life, "how the hell did that happen? Huskies are going to eat well tonight!" And with that they wandered off laughing through the ice fog. Poor old Boris, he fitted in around here as much as I did.

I pushed open the heavy door of the hotel and entered a dimly lit, smoky room filled with laughter and music. Through the haze I saw Bridge serving drinks, squeezing between the tables carrying a tray of beer above her head with her left hand. She was chatting and laughing with anybody she passed. She looked every inch the working girl of the north, still wearing her size five Doc Martins and little black dress.

Bridge had found a cabin for us to live in on the other side of the river, which right now might as well have been in Bognor Regis because the river was impassable. Icebergs so large the captain of the Titanic would have seen them, were travelling at 10 miles an hour down the river. They filled every inch of steaming water and crashed into each other with alarming Hollywood sound affects.

We stayed in town for a couple of days and felt the temperature plummet to -35°C. It was during this time in town that I realised my wife had made quite an impression on the local gents in my absence. In a town of four men to one woman a Galapagos Marine Iguana, female or not, would make a fine mate. Consequently, Bridge had stirred up the sort of testosterone only seen in professional wrestling. Bridge tried hard to introduce me to some of the local colour as we ran into them around town but all they said was, "oh, you're the guy we've got to kill." This was not the sort of adventure I really needed. These men were hard, rough and used to fighting to survive. I, on the other hand, was soft, cuddly and used to surviving by putting it on plastic.

We couldn't wait to get out of town and into our cabin, and luckily the last couple of days at 30 below were just what was needed. It slowed the river enough to jam the ice burgs together on a slow bend just south of the town. As soon as the ice looked passable, Boris and I made our way out of town on foot towards the ice jam, while Bridge stayed behind to work.

I had never seen anything like it. Huge chunks of ice 4 to 6 feet thick were crushed together rising out of the river like mountains. Open patches of dark water steamed like hot springs in a chilling turmoil. I picked my way carefully across the jam using an axe to test the thickness of the ice while Boris scrambled with shaking legs behind me. Sometimes we had to jump, from one burgh to the next, to avoid deep holes where water churned below.

After realising that the ice was, in places, thick enough to saunter over Boris's enthusiasm grew and while I took my time to find a firm footing, Boris charged across the river with tail and ears flapping as if waving farewell to a loved one in a rapidly departing train. Inevitably he disappeared, helped by the force of gravity and the sort of stupidity you find in a professional bungy jumper. I found him whimpering at the bottom of an ice crevice, his head was below his backside and his tail was the only thing I had a chance of grabbing. Swallowing my anger, I choked out a "good boy Boris!" which encouraged him to wag his tail. I grabbed it and hauled him out screaming like a newborn. He again took off, apparently deaf, and I was left shouting into the cold.

I finally made it out of the jam and onto the shore ice on the other side. We had to follow the shore for about a mile and then cut up through the woods where a creek joined the river. The shore ice was flatter and much easier going, but then I heard a crack. I looked down and all around my feet large white cracks shot out in all directions. I began to worry and shuffled my feet further apart only to see more cracks appearing. It was at this moment Einstein (aka Boris) decided to return with his ears flapping and tail still wagging. Only good at hearing the dull chime of his food bowl, he ignored my pleas to 'stay', came running up and promptly sank through the ice, taking me with him.

The water was only knee high but so cold that I'm sure my yodels could be heard in Ottawa. I dragged Boris by the scruff of the neck through the water and out onto thicker ice. We were both wet and howling, but I know my (albeit unprintable) howling was more eloquent.

It was a real shock to feel the unstoppable cold in my feet. I thought hard about what to do next. It would take an hour or more to get back across the river and then I had a 4 mile walk back to town. Judging by my hand drawn map, I was closer to the cabin than town. I had matches so should be able to make a fire once I found it. Unsure if I was doing the right thing, I trudged on.

The sun was dropping and the sky was an incredible array of blues and purples. The spruce on the hills around were silhouettes as the shadows crept out of the valleys and up the cliff sides. Walking became harder. My feet were numb and my trousers frozen solid to my shins. I stumbled over ice blocks, unable to feel my feet touch the ground. For the first time in my life, before eight pints of Fosters and a spicy curry, I had to walk visually.

I found a small track leading up from the river valley and followed it beside a once vibrant creek, which had been halted in mid-flow by extreme temperatures. I could see the iced ripples and flow of the water as it once negotiated rocks and fallen trees.

The creek wound its way down through the silent forest. I entered a black and white world. The fresh snow that clung to the trees, in heaps, was so white it drained the green from the trees, making them appear black, blocking out the spectrum of colours in the sky.

The track seemed to be going nowhere and the spruce trees were closing in. Covered with thick blankets of snow, some leaned completely over with the weight. Just as it was almost dark I saw a small log cabin in a clearing through the trees, half buried in snow. I waded through the snow and up the wooden steps. A frozen broom stood on the porch, a small log pile was neatly stacked next to the door.

The door creaked open on frozen hinges revealing a single room with a big black cast-iron stove in one corner. A few homemade cupboards lined one wall and a plain table and two chairs stood in the centre. A small pile of logs already split was neatly stacked next to the stove, and the fire was laid ready for lighting. It is common practice in the north to always leave the fire ready to light before you depart, because you never know who will need it quickly when they find sanctuary in your cabin during the winter. I fumbled with cold hands in my pocket for a match, struck it on the cast iron stove and popped it into the firebox. Seconds later the crackling of fire and the creaking of cold metal warming could be heard. Half an hour later the stove was spreading life, giving warmth and Boris, shaking and whimpering, crawled over to it and nestled down to rid his belly of ice.

Once I stopped moving I became unbearably cold and started to shake. My brain knew what it wanted my fingers to do but they went into slow motion and curled up like bacon on the barbie. The concentration it took just to get my boots off would have got me through four years of university. My poor feet finally felt the warmth of the fire as I pushed them onto the stove, until I could smell the burning of my socks. I dragged a chair over and huddled as close as I could next to the stove. Boris worked hard to rid the ice from his fur and fought with me for prime space next to the fire. It was surprising how quickly the frozen cabin warmed up. It creaked and groaned as the warmth touched the frozen logs.

I sat for several hours next to the fire singeing the hair off my legs until my body relaxed enough to reconnect with my brain. I looked around the dark cabin. The firelight danced along the floor and across the ceiling beams, and nails driven into the logs for coat hooks threw long black shadows across the golden logs. Was this place really going to be our home for the winter, a sanctuary to comfort us in harsh weather? Or was it a padded cell keeping the incapable and obviously insane from harm and protecting us from the real world? Only time would tell.

A couple of days later we had moved out of Dawson City and into our home in the woods. Accessing the cabin would have made Sir Edmund Hilary plan for a month and take a few extra gurkers with him, so it had taken several gruelling trips back and forth with heavy packs to complete our move. The only way up to the cabin was along the frozen creek that joined the river. It was littered with rocks and boulders, covered in a glacier that grew daily and all up hill. Walking in the cold weather didn't help - breathing was painful, and ice on our eyelids made it difficult to see boulders that could easily twist an ankle.

Getting supplies back from town was a continuing ordeal and it quickly became obvious that we needed transport of some kind. Food was expensive in town and we had to be careful what we bought. Fresh vegetables were totally out of the question, not only because we couldn't get any in Dawson, except perhaps the sort of wrinkled, mummified carrots we sometimes found in the back of our fridge back home, but also because they froze quickly on the way home. Tinned food also spoiled on freezing and the tins often split. Meat was priced like you would expect in a town where 98% of people go shopping in the wilderness with a high powered rifle and a frisky moose call; and only bought a chicken thigh when they needed chicken bait for their traps. Which is never, because any self-respecting North American predator has no idea what a chicken is.

We'd had to park Pricey for the winter, because she flatly refused to move in the cold and her door handles, hinges, and tailgates were snapping off with alarming regularity. We decided to get a snowmobile, the main form of transport around here in the winter - basically a motorbike with skis. We had enough money to buy a cheap second hand one, and as there were very few to be had in Dawson in the depth of winter, all we had to do was wait until one came up for sale.

One particularly cold afternoon I was sheltering from the weather in the comforts of the bar contemplating how people actually survived up here. All around me numerous 'everyday' conversations were being held, studded with statements like, "well I never did find my finger", "we found his tracks but they disappeared under the ice", "I went to rub his ear for him and it snapped right off", "my hair was frozen for four days". Interrupting my eavesdropping a weather beaten French chap sidled up to me in a fur coat and said he had a snow machine for sale. When I expressed an interest, he babbled incessantly about carbides, independent suspension, torque, paddle tracks and liquid cooled, so to shut him up I went outside to have a look. I put on my, 'Yeah, but I didn't want a blue one' face, but all I could really think about was the long cold, hike home. After ten minutes of bartering I bought it, solely because it was the only one for sale. Life is so simple in the north.

With my supersonic speedy Skidoo between our legs we were now mobile, and frozen. And was I frozen. It was unbelievably cold on a fast moving machine with no windbreak at 30 below and I literally froze my face off. After several trips the skin on my nose and cheeks peeled off, leaving open sores that were incredibly painful. My ears shed more skin than an adolescent adder. I had to sleep on my back because anything touching my face was excruciating. In town everybody laughed. I might as well have hung a placard around my neck saying 'novice southerner'.

We were finding everything in our day to day living very hard and overwhelming. We had to completely relearn how to live, how to walk and how to dress. We didn't have any real winter clothes and we hadn't learnt how to wear the clothes we had to stop ourselves from sweating and to keep the wind out. We had bought a few trendy items that we thought were winter clothes but they turned out to be useful in Edmonton if you had to run from the car to your house. Up here the warmest clothing is animal skins, and most people make their own mittens, hats and moccasins out of passing bears that stop for a moose steak hanging in their meat shed.

My frozen face was a serious injury that even today I feel. But the hardy northern heroes weren't laughing at my new appearance, they were laughing at my ignorance, of venturing north and thinking I could survive on my wits alone. Every time I went into town I received an onslaught of macho bullshit and was the subject of many bets to see if I would be dead or south by spring. I probably deserved it, but was determined to prove them wrong.

December 1999

With an average temperature of 28 below since we moved into the cabin, we were becoming tired of the struggle just to keep comfortable. We had never been in temperatures like these, never mind living and trying to survive week after week in them. It was like being surrounded by heaven but living in purgatory. We could feel the beauty, taste the adventure and embrace the freedom around us but we lived a never-ending battle to be comfortable, warm and safe. We resigned ourselves to the fact that it would take a long time before we learnt the rules of the magical north. Probably just as long as it had for the rugged macho men who laughed at us through their bushy beards and weather worn faces, because most of them started out in life, just like we did, below the 60th parallel.

Even so, living in a forest gripped by winter was the most amazing experience. It is difficult to describe the beauty and tranquility. First of all, there is complete silence, a silence you can almost hear. With that there is a total stillness, one that stretches to the top of white, jagged mountains, into deep valleys and through the endless forest. There is almost an understanding by the northern world that the beauty of the winter must not be spoilt, so everything stands motionless, as if the environment is holding something delicate in its hands.

There is nobody around for hundreds of miles. You can go to any hill and sit at night under a perfectly clear, unpolluted sky and see forever into the horizon. The stars are so big, you can almost touch them and they really do shine. The moon and the constellations cast a bright silver light across the wilderness and throw dark blue, contorted shadows onto the sparkling snow. High on the horizon the Ogilvie Mountains snake their way north, standing like the teeth on the lower jaw of a wolf. The snow on their sides reflects the sun's moods with an amazing spectrum of pastel yellows, pinks and blues. Shadows in their canyons suggest hidden worlds where in all probability no man has ever set foot.

Snow muffles every sound in the woods. It coats every branch and twig on the dark spruce which becomes so winter-weary that it bows to the snow beneath it and is suspended in time like a mime artist acting out a slow motion drama. The smaller willows and poplars become intricate snow sculptures as the snow falls on their delicate forms. You can hear the silence all around you. You dare not tread in unbroken snow because you feel you will taint it forever.

In this world a moment is precious, and life is on the edge. You can walk along a trail one day and see tall mature spruce that have thrived for hundreds of years. The next day you can walk the same trail and see the spruce crippled and broken by the heavy snow. All around us are reminders of our mortality. The bitter cold doesn't suffers fools and misadventure, the gusting wind can turn a routine trip to town into a survival situation, freezing your skin, blinding you with snow and hiding the trail in minutes. (As I sit here writing this I am mourning a friend who drowned in the turbulent water below the ice on the river two nights ago).

We live with the tilt of the earth. As the days pass and we

move towards spring, the sun begins to flirt with the snow-covered spruce, lighting their tops like expensive Christmas candles. The dance with the sun is a little longer each day. It's the only real way of telling the passing of time. I go for walks alone most days to search for land on which to build our home, and almost cry on every one because of the flawless beauty around me.

Because the winter sun sits low on the horizon it makes the sky a constant mix of colours. On the far horizon a blue tinge slowly melts into an array of gentle warming colours until it reaches the sun and liquefies into a deep red. Before we came here we heard of the long dark winters from people who had never been here. It's true that for six weeks between early December and into January light only tantalises the world for 4 to 6 hours a day, but nothing was said of the amazing, all day sunrises and sunsets that occur for most of the winter. Nobody told us about the rainbows you see in the valleys when a slight wind carries ice crystals from the trees and into the clear sky.

Inside our cabin there is no running water, electricity, radio, mirrors, clocks, locks, or phone. There is nothing except what we really need. We spend night after night reading to each other over candlelight, accompanied by the crackle of the fire, its shadows dancing on the ceiling. We are not shouted at by a television, so we don't worry about rushing out and buying the latest toilet paper or oven cleaner. I don't worry about going to work or about time, for it has no purpose here. Instead, everybody and everything tends to be governed by the weather. Most people in the bush get up when it's light and are in their cabins tucking into a pot of caribou stew by the time dusk arrives. If the temperature drops below -40°C it is dangerous to venture far from home, so only the people in town go to work. Others do so when it is safe.

There's a lot of work just keeping our place livable. Firewood has to be cut and split, snow has to be melted for water, meals and trips to town take days to plan. Bridge and I work together, and with that comes a true understanding that we've never reached before. We've simply touched a finger on each others face and warmed a white frozen cheek or nose that the other didn't know was frozen. That is a remarkable loving thing. It's almost religious, and to me one of the many perfect everyday moments. I can't help looking at Bridge as somebody I must protect and love. But she is a strong lady and in such a hard world as this we both protect and love each other equally. We have developed a higher awareness of how the other person is - how they're feeling, how they're struggling. For this we feel so lucky.

Bridge decided to keep her job during the winter, so needed to make a journey into town three days a week, which was an adventure in itself. Not just because we had to remember which days she had to work but also what the time was every morning. We could tell roughly within an hour by the shadows on the snow outside, and if it was light when we awoke, we knew she was several hours late because it didn't get light until 10.30 a.m. for a lot of the winter. Like most jobs in Dawson, Bridge worked flexible hours so it wasn't too crucial that she arrived exactly at 9.00 a.m. She had to cross the partly frozen river twice a day, in the dark and on her own. The ice shifts and sinks throughout the winter causing the river to flow over it - this 'overflow' could be several feet deep and difficult to distinguish from the deep open water. It was quite an experience waving goodbye to Bridge as she sped off on the skidoo through the trees, leaving me totally without contact until she returned 10 hours later. I often had to stop myself walking into town just to see if she made it or not. The river appears to drown at least one person from Dawson every year. Although Bridge was scared every time she drove onto the ice she hardly showed it. It was something we had to get used to, like fighting for space on the underground or queuing in traffic jams or bus stops.

The day Bridge didn't return from work I was as psychotic as a London driver in rush hour. I kept telling myself she was only a few hours late, as I waited for the faint flicker of the skidoo light to shine through the trees. I knew a minute seemed like an hour in these situations so I chopped the nights' wood, cooked the evening meal and shouted at the dog until finally I could stand it no longer.

I grabbed my coat, flung open the cabin door and went into the moonlit woods like a superhero from a telephone box. I cut down our trail and onto the river. I had only walked a little way on the ice when a light flickered way down river. A couple of minutes later Bridge rode up on the skidoo. She was fine and decidedly chipper for someone who had dropped their skidoo through the ice on the Klondike river, had to climb out, walk back to town, dry off, warm up, get help, pull the skidoo from the freezing water, chip ice from the engine, under carriage and track, thaw it out and get it going again, just so she could come home and try it all over again tomorrow in the dark. I on the other hand was shaken up but I tried not to show it. I squinted at the horizon and rubbed my stubbly chin. "Shit Happens!," I said. "How was work, honey?"

January 2000

In January the whole world stopped moving and froze. All the years of planning to see in a new millennium with style, on top of a hill looking over the ocean, or under Big Ben, or on the beach in New Zealand, seemed so far away. All we could do was huddle under the blankets in a desperate attempt to keep warm. It was amazing the difference the really cold weather made to our living conditions. At -20°C we had sat out on the deck drinking hot chocolate. We'd been wrapped up in winter clothes but it was comfortable. The cabin was warm and didn't need much wood to keep it that way. But when the temperature dropped well below -45°C life became bizarre. For the whole of January we were confined to our cabin and had the ride of our lives. Our cozy cabin suddenly became a glorified icebox. Every food item we had stored froze in the cupboards. Our twenty feet by twenty feet living space shrunk to 2 feet from the stove. We dragged the bed up to the stove and cuddled under the blankets while we watched frost creep up the cast iron base of the stove until it was inches from the firebox. The door to the cabin became encrusted with 2 inches of frost. The washing up water in the bowl on the counter froze, ice gathered in between the logs on the walls, our boots froze to the floor, the windows froze completely over and anything remotely mechanical did not even begin to turn over.

It was dangerous to wander too far from the cabin but important to keep busy because cabin fever was always a day away. One of the jobs I had been putting off for ages was cleaning the outhouse, a three sided log structure in the clump of birch trees just behind our cabin. Usually we cleaned it by simply knocking the frozen turd pyramid over with the pickaxe, but after a couple of months it was pretty full. We had been told that shooting it with a high powered rifle disperses everything nicely.

One cold winter morning, not a bird noting my passing, I nervously pushed over-hanging branches aside and made my way down the isolated path to the outhouse wall. I stood tall, puffed out my chest, cocked my rifle and chewed the butt of my cigar. A dirty job had to be done and I was the only one to do it. Without hesitation I shoved the barrel into the hole and fired a volley of shots that echoed in the surrounding hills. Mission accomplished.

It wasn't until I was back with Bridge by the fire that we smelt something was amiss. Boris was outside, so it wasn't him. Running my fingers through my hair I realised I was wearing most of the outhouse, and that it had now thawed.

February 2000

During the really cold spell our skidoo was frozen solid. We'd had to once again revert to the tried and tested method of putting one foot in front of the other for transport. It seems so typical of the way of life in the north. Just when you really need something it doesn't work. A lot of people here run dog sleds as a reliable form of transport. It was the dogs that opened up the North, delivered the mail and brought in supplies. They are always keen to run and never break down, so after the normal amount of thought I put into these things I decided to get a dog team. It seemed logical and practical from the comfort of the cabin. We would have reliable transport no matter what the weather and anyway, how hard could it be?

I went to see a neighbour who lived with his wife in a 16-foot square cabin a couple of miles away through the trees. Brent was a very relaxed, quietly spoken chap in his thirties, and was only too keen to help. I had never met him before but without hesitation he lent me a team of ten dogs and a sled. I hastily explained that the only thing I knew about dogs was that they leave a mess on the pavement and bury chop bones in your roses. He smiled kindly and assured me it wasn't rocket science, but seeing a concerned look creep over my face and daylight through my ears he offered to give me a few lessons on some of the trails through the nearby bush.

There must have been over thirty dogs in Brent's dog yard. Some were big broad huskies, others were smaller, faster dogs bred especially for long distant racing. They all jumped enthusiastically and barked excitedly on the end of their chains as we walked amongst them. You could tell at an instant that Brent loved his dogs. The yard was spotless with not a single doggy pooh in sight. Their kennels were lined neatly in rows and stuffed with copious amounts of fresh, clean straw. Every dog was fit and healthy with a shine in their eyes that told of their adventures on the trail.

Brent wandered through the yard pointing out individual dogs. "This is Batman, he's a pain in the rear but he runs like the wind. This is Draco, stupid mutt insists on peeing in his food bowl. This is Whiskey, she's run the Yukon Quest twice." He rubbed each dog on the head as it reared up to greet him, exuding love and proud to be noticed in the crowd. "This is Homer Simpson. He's a right ass, I named him right!" The dog's individual personalities were striking. Billy, a lead dog, howled into the air because we were taking our time getting to her. Dingo jumped around in circles on the end of her chain, excited because she had visitors. Bart hid in his kennel - he was old and retired and didn't want to run today.

My team was made up of six veterans and four younger dogs. I tried to remember their names but it was pretty difficult to catch them, as Brent's quiet voice was quickly lost amongst the chorus of excited dogs. When Brent started to hook up dogs to two sleds the dogs erupted, dancing on the end of their chains with all the style of Michael Jackson in tight leather trousers. They knew what was coming and couldn't wait. I helped Brent hook up the eager dogs one by one. Once harnessed they jumped and strained at the reigns, desperate to get going. Brent put on his gloves, pulled his hood up and shouted to me "The first corner out of the dog yard is a little bit tricky so watch what I do, if I don't make it try something different." And with that he pulled his snow anchor (a large, aggressive-looking metal hook) out of the snow and sped off around the corner. I watched in disbelief. The speed of ten dogs was incredible and Brent had hung onto the sled as if it were a Tesco's shopping trolley full of stolen fruit and veg on a very steep hill.

My team saw him go and frantically tried to follow. Nervously, I put my gloves on and stood on the back of the sled. This only increased the dogs' enthusiasm and they began to pull the sled, slowly dragging the snow hook through the snow. I bent down and tried to pull the hook. The pressure of ten crazy dogs feeling the need for speed on the end of it made it impossible to pull out. The dogs were jumping impatiently into the air on the end of their harnesses. I had to get moving and quickly before a fight broke out. I took my gloves off, stood off the sled, braced myself and yanked at the snow hook with both hands. It came free. The instant the dogs felt a slight give in the line they took off at break-neck speed. I dived for the rapidly departing sled and managed to grab the handrail.

My feet were searching blindly for the runner stands as the soles of my boots left the skid mark of a formula one car on the snow. My startled gaze was rigidly fixed on the rapidly approaching hairpin corner. A split second later the lead dogs took the corner. I tried to adopt a similar stance to Brent but only succeeded in standing as if I was trying to give birth to an over due African elephant and steered the sled directly into a tree. The sled tipped over, taking me with it, but didn't slow the dogs one bit. My scrambled brain remembered Brents' words, "Whatever happens, don't let go of the sled, or we'll be looking for the team in Alaska for days." I hung onto the handrail while my nose filled up with snow. "It's all right," I repeated to myself, "no one's watching," as I was dragged unceremoniously through the snow. Coming to my senses I realised that the heavy object in my hood was in fact the snow hook. This was the only means I had of stopping the dogs. I tried to reach it but the sled bounced off the trail, into deep snow and through several bushes as the dogs decided to hunt a snow shoe hare taking a short cut through the thick bush.

My jacket ballooned with snow as the sled thumped into every tree and through all sorts of Triffid-like bushes. I was just about to let go and book a ticket to Alaska when the snow became deeper and the sled harder to pull. The dogs slowed and stopped.

Wondering how I was going to keep the wild promises I had just made to the Almighty, I clambered to my feet and caught my breath while the dogs looked around wondering what the hold up was. With real insight as to why someone invented the combustion engine, I righted the sled. Big mistake. The dogs took off again with incredible power. I again leapt for the sled and this time managed to stay upright. We bumped over tree stumps beneath the snow, rounded fallen logs and through snowdrifts without even the slightest hint of reduced speed. Eventually we turned onto a trail that wound its way up the side of a hill. With the initial charge over with and faced with a hill the dogs slowed to a pace that brought my cheeks back from my ears. This gave me a little time to gather my shattered nerves, untangle the snow hook from my hood and dig it into the snow to bring them to a relatively controlled stop.

Brent was nowhere to be seen. He was long gone and probably wandering what was keeping me. I undid my coat to release the snow from the inside, put my gloves on, checked my Y-fronts and reluctantly prepared myself for another NASA take off.

I was obviously taking too long in catching my breath and controlling my shakes. The lead dogs decided they were having a far better time chasing the elusive snow shoe hare than dragging a stunned pommy up a hill. They promptly turned and ran back past the sled, dragging the whole team with them. I jumped off the sled and grabbed them by the collars, which stopped the lead dogs but not the rest of the team, who danced a maypole routine around my legs. I frantically tried to untangle the mayhem when Draco, obviously missing his food bowl, cocked his leg and peed into Dingo's' ear. Dingo found this a little distressing and started a fight, which then sparked the sort of brawl you get when a bar full of drunken sailors start singing.

It was a mess! Dogs biting and snarling at each other, lines getting more and more tangled around me. I couldn't move because my shins were trusted up like a hapless chicken on a Sunday. I tried to stay on my feet but was toppled by Batman.

It took me quite a while to stop the fighting without getting bitten myself. But finally I had untangled the dogs and put them in a straight line in front of the sled. I was just getting the lead dogs into position when again they took off. This time the sled came whizzing into me, knocking me off my feet. The next couple of moments are a little bit hazy but I came to sitting in the sleds' carriage, inches from the snow, totally helpless and far away from the braking system while the dogs had great fun charging off through the woods out of control. I was exhausted and shaking like a leaf. 'What happens now?' I thought as we careered off through the trees. I scrambled to my knees, climbed around the back of the sled and onto the runners, where I hung like a drowning man to a life jacket as the dogs ran for mile after mile through unfamiliar bush.

Several hours later the dogs turned into Brents' Driveway and came to a stop in the yard to a chorus of howling. Brent came out of the cabin, drinking a hot chocolate and looking extremely relaxed and warm. I on the other hand was frozen stiff, extremely shocked and looked like a cross between a battered Christmas ornament and Dracos' food bowl. "You'd better thank the dogs." Brent said bending to pat my team. I wanted to reach for the gun and shoot a leg off each of them but thought I'd better not.

The next couple of days we tried again and each time I ended up slightly less frazzled and bruised, until it reached a point where the scenery passed with silence. The only noise as we travelled through the winter woods was the panting of the dogs, the occasional chime of their buckles and the runners on the frosted snow. It was magical, and I quickly became aware that the trick wasn't rocket science, just a lot of doggy biscuits.

Fresh meat was high on our 'wish list' in the middle of January. If we had been in Dawson in the autumn, we would've been able to get a moose for our winter meat supply just like most other people here. But we hadn't, and our diet of tinned vegetables and over-priced pork chops was crippling us in more ways than one. When Brent suggested we go on a caribou hunt, to stock up on supplies, I jumped at the chance.

Well before it was light one cold, January morning Brent and I loaded his truck with the skidoo, a couple of rifles, survival kits and a packed lunch and left for the formidable Tombstone Mountains. Several hours later while the sky flamed red we were climbing the mountain road to where we thought the caribou would be over-wintering. In this part of the Yukon there are two distinct herds of caribou. There are about 10,000 of the Forty Mile herd and they live in the woods around the border of Alaska and the Yukon. We were looking for a transient herd, the famous Porcupine Caribou, that wander the barren lands and the arctic throughout the winter.

We parked the truck on the side of the track and studied the herd through binoculars against the mountain backdrop, it was like a scene from a snow-covered Serengeti. I had only seen the Tombstone Mountains from a distance and even then they'd looked bleak and uninviting. From where I sat now in the comforts of the truck, watching the wind whip up the snow and part the thick winter fur on the caribou's flanks, they looked more hostile than ever.

We needed to be quick to catch up with the herd. The

wind nearly blew us over when we got out of the truck, and numbed our fingers while we struggled to put on gloves and facemasks. We dropped into the deep snow and hugged the contours of the land to begin our approach. The knee- high snow made our progress painfully slow.

We stayed down wind from the herd so our civilized stench didn't reach the raw, beautiful animals. We stopped moving every time an animal looked up and continued our stalk only when it had started feeding again. It was vital to get close for a good shot and a clean kill, so we took our time to make certain our approach went unnoticed. Their splendour was unmistakable. Long, powerful legs and wide padded feet to carry them elegantly through the drifting snow. Dense winter coats, dark brown along the back and flanks, blending into pure white from the shoulders to the head. Dark chestnut eyes sparkling in the sun. The bulls' majestic curved antlers with twisted tines raked the sky when they walked.

As they have done for thousands of years, the caribou travel across hundreds of miles of desolate terrain to winter in the Tombstone valleys. Evidence of their passage is everywhere - deep grooves worn into riverbanks and the sides of mountains, discarded antlers littering the tundra like weapons on a battlefield after conflict. The ecosystem was entwined with their way of life.

Only the occasional cough or sigh drifted on the wind as the caribou wandered. We used natural rises in the rolling land to hide our approach to a nearby group. Once within killing distance, we studied the herd again through binoculars for the right targets. Three unfortunate animals stood out. A young bull, perhaps two years old, and two calf-less females. Not only would their meat not be tough like the large bulls but their loss wouldn't damage the intricate structure of the herd. They were big enough to feed us for the winter, and, to be blunt, they were expendable.

We nestled into the snow about a 100 yards from our chosen targets and raised our rifles. Through the scope of the rifle the beauty and softness of these creatures was profound. Every hair on their hides reflected the sun, every purposeful movement echoed centuries of movement before them. As I studied the young male, knowing I was going to kill it at any moment, I started to have second thoughts. I wasn't starving so why should I take him? But then if I were starving I wouldn't be able to make it into these mountains and get food. Meat in the supermarket packaged in styrofoam trays and wrapped in cling film looks like meat, and definitely not like a vital part of a fluffy, white lamb springing around green fields dotted with yellow daffodils bobbing in the breeze. Try as I might, staring at this most glorious, perfect, gentle animal in its natural environment of endless snow I couldn't look at it as a pound of sausages.

A cacophonic crack echoed around the mountains and one of the females slumped forward with her head in the snow. As the remnants of life drained from her body, her back legs wobbled then collapsed, felling her carcass into the snow. Brent had shot first and put the bullet exactly where he wanted it for a quick kill.

The other caribou looked up from their foraging, saw the lifeless body of the female twitching in the snow beside them, then returned to their feeding. Which put things back into perspective. This species was armed with a multitude of instincts that protected them from shock or trauma. As long as they couldn't detect us, they wouldn't associate dead Doris bleeding all over the snow next to them as a hint of possible trouble. Unless they actually see the cause of death, they don't flee for safety but continue with what they're doing.

Another loud shot rang out and the other female slumped into the snow, but stood back up and struggled forward a few paces. Brent shot again and her neck exploded as the bullet ripped through her flesh. She stood for a few seconds with her head in the snow, then she became unsteady and collapsed. "Go on, shoot", whispered Brent as I lay in the snow with the cross hairs of the scope on the chest of the young bull. I didn't want to tell him that I had trouble putting a worm on a fishing hook, never mind killing such a perfect creature.

I took a deep breath and focused in on the bull once more. Adrenaline was shaking my body as I tried desperately to steady the rifle for the shot. I squeezed the trigger and for a split second everything around me went silent and dark. I opened my eyes to see the bull drop to its haunches, where it stayed. I was horrified. Its head was still up and it looked as if it had sat down for a rest.

We sprang from cover and ran through the snow to the targets, scattering other caribou. We reached the two females first. One was dead, the other was lying in the snow blinking at us with dark brown eyes as she tried hard to draw breath through her splintered neck. Behind them the young bull sat in the snow, now stained red around its body, watching us with terrified eyes. A hole the size of a football in its belly was spewing the bulls' last, half-digested meal onto the snow every time the poor animal coughed. It tried to climb to its feet and make a final dash for safety. We had to leave the dying female and concentrate on the bull. It would have been disastrous if it ran off injured and had to suffer a long painful death. I ran closer. The bull clambered to its feet and looked for a place to run. I raised my rifle and shot him in the head. A split second later he was gone. Only a twitching, lifeless, carcass was left in the blood red snow. We ran back to the female but she too had gone. She now stared back at us with a vacant, motionless eye.

I sank to my knees and took a deep breath as I stared at the poor creatures we had destroyed. The sun was setting in a purple haze framed by tall white mountains on the horizon, but next to me lay death. I didn't feel proud of myself and fought off guilt as we dragged the carcasses together. I was relieved it was over though, and the thought that we wouldn't waste their lives calmed me. In front of me was at least six months worth of good wholesome meat and three skins that could be made into winter clothes.

The chilling wind was rapidly freezing the carcasses, as well as ourselves, so it was important to gut the animals and get them back to the truck as soon as possible. "This is where we earn our meat." Brent said, unsheathing his knife. We split open the bellies and pulled out the guts in a vale of steam. We drained what blood we could and dragged the bodies back through the deep snow, leaving the gut piles for the wolves.

It was about an hour back to the truck and we dragged in silence, watching the night arrive in a spectrum of deep blues and purples while the wind hid our tracks and the bloodstains with fresh snow. We were sweating and exhausted when we reached the truck, and the caribou looked as if they had never been alive. Their eyes were pale and dry, their pristine coats bloodstained and caked with snow and their limbs ridged.

Back at the cabin I hung the young bull's frozen body from the roof of the wood shed. The head fixed to one side as it lay in the sawdust on the floor. A dim candle, melting on a nearby stack of wood, threw a faint light onto the flank of the carcass, sparkling the bloodstained snow matted in the hide. I rested a hand on the shoulder and whispered a low and sincere thank you.

By mid February daylight was lasting for nine hours. The coldest, darkest and hardest part of the winter was behind us and we had managed to scrape through relatively unscathed. We had quickly learned not to plan anything too far ahead or to fight the weather, for the weather ruled this land worse than a temperamental dictator. We had learnt through necessity to cope with the extreme conditions and had carved a fairly relaxed and considerably more comfortable life for ourselves. We had developed systems to collect snow for water, to have enough firewood for several weeks and to dry heavy winter clothes so they were fresh for the next jaunt into the woods.

With the really cold temperatures came a glorious, crisp, winter sunshine and sparkling clear nights, and with them came the waltz of the northern lights, that danced across their stage like a world class, Russian ballet. It was refreshing to feel the biting cold on our skin and see the country bathed in blinding sunshine.

March 2000

My dog running had become second nature, and I now understood the logic and beauty of this timeless form of travel. The dogs were always keen to run and eager to please even when they had to pull a sled heavy with supplies or camping equipment, and to be at one with them on a lonely trail was awesome. They are companions that can be trusted with your life, and with them leading, it was almost certain you would get home. The worry of being stranded or lost diminished with every one of their steps.

I got to know each member of the team very quickly and could tell at a glance if they were tiring, hungry or just pleased to be on the trail. Billy was the main leader, a veteran of many long distant races across the north. She had the gentle, quiet way of an elderly scholar, filling in her twilight years by teaching school children about a subject she knew well and loved with a passion. Her partner in the line was Angus, also a veteran of many races, but who thinks he knows it all and would often lead the pack on his own chosen route. This made Billy glance round at me and howl in frustration.

Frazer and Bea were next in line, brother and sister with a loving close bond. They wagged their whole bodies enthusiastically when I approached, and to help my inexperienced hands put on their harnesses would lift their feet one at a time and duck their heads. I never had any trouble with these two. They were exceptional dogs with endless patience. Though it did concern me slightly that Frazer insisted on cocking his leg against Bea so she was always encrusted with frozen pee.

Dingo and Draco were next and continually fought, which was mainly down to the young, fearsome Dingo. She was so highly-strung and enthusiastic that if we stopped for a moment she raised hell in the ranks and wound Draco up into a frothing beast. He often came back from a run covered in blood because Dingo insisted on biting his ear as they ran.

The next two dogs were Albert and Batman. Albert was a very shy individual and shook nervously while he was hooked up. But once on the run he transformed into an amazing athlete. Batman ran like the wind and I often watched him on the hills, straining with all his might to pull the heavy sled over the rise.

Spook and Roxy were closest to the sled. Roxy was an old dog that often tried to get out of pulling. She loved to run fast and would save her energy on the hills, preferring the faster descent on the other side. I would call to her to 'pick it up a bit' and she would look around hoping I wasn't talking to her. When she was certain I was she would pull a little way, only to revert to her easier pace a moment later. Spook was a big, white dog and Roxy's son. He was a trifle dim and thought only with his John Thomas. He insisted on trying to mount every member of the team when we stopped, female or not. In fact he didn't seem to care from what end he tried and I was forever stopping him from trying to make love to Roxy's ear.

A team of ten dogs can pull a 6000-pound truck out of a ditch, and on every run I was amazed at their power. I could venture further into the bush looking for land without fear of the skidoo breaking down or getting stuck. The dogs really opened up the country for me, and I covered endless, silent miles of motionless wilderness with only the dogs as company.

Sometimes on clear moonlit nights Brent and I would go on a midnight run far off into the dormant, silver hills. Our shadows cast by the moon stretched across the snow. When the chill of the night became uncomfortable we would travel back through forgotten valleys and over windswept hills to Dawson, whose lights shone out of the dark river valley like dying embers in a neglected campfire.

April 2000

One morning we awoke to the sound of water dripping, a sound we had not heard since before moving into the cabin over six months before. The warm spring sun, which now shone for 14 hours a day, was melting the snow on the cabin roof. Water droplets shone like jewels as they clung to the spikes of the icicles hanging from the eves. We had long since retired the dogs for the season because the weather was now too warm to run. With their thick winter coats the dogs quickly overheat in temperatures averaging -2°C. It was amazing how warm it felt after the brutal winter. Bridge insisted on wearing her little black dress and walked around as if she was off to a village fete in July, and I must admit I'd even taken my jumper off.

The dripping sound was welcome but also strangely disappointing. The winter had been a struggle but it had flown by and we'd never been bored. Every day was filled with little adventures or problems. We were just getting the hang of walking in snowshoes (misery slippers as they are called up here) and Boris had the area around our cabin decorated the way he liked it. Now all too quickly it was over. There would be no more skidooing, breaking trail and cold crisp winter nights. No more northern lights dancing around a dark, star studded sky, no more glorious pastel skies, no more dog sledding and no more long evenings by a fire in the cozy cabin. Soon we would have to prepare for 'break-up', a term given to the river thawing. It was still almost a month away but already we could feel the pressure of a different adventure.

Money had been low on our list of priorities because we could live without it for long periods of time in the bush.

A trapper from the Tombstones had told me he had several $100 dollar bills in his cabin with dust on them. He had even been tempted to light the fire with them on the really cold nights when he had no kindling. Even so, we had empty cupboards and our clothes were disintegrating fast. It was time for a little injection of cash.

I found a job working for a colourful Dutchman on his gold mine deep up the Indian River. With the snow melting fast he wanted to get a head start on stripping the topsoil to the 'pay dirt'. I said I'd give him a few weeks but couldn't work longer than that because I had a life to live. He was used to that sort of answer and took me on. I stayed in a run-down bush camp on the Indian river and we toiled in the mud for three weeks, stripping the frozen top soil and exposing the gravel of an ancient river bed where he knew the gold lay in waiting.

Our efforts not only exposed the gravel but also an assortment of mammoth bones and a prehistoric beaver skeleton. Finding relics of the prehistoric age was much more exciting than discovering gold, but the bones were discarded like waste gravel. This land is so untouched it is still possible to walk where no one has ever been before and to regularly discover important links to the past. Anywhere else such relics would have been in museums for decades, mused over by boffins in white coats, spotted bow ties and hair cuts that look like they've been given life with electricity.

May 2000

Once back at the cabin, my pockets bulging with wanga we began to plan for break-up. The snow had melted quickly and we were rediscovering lost items including a knife some, spanners and $25 that had been hidden by the white blanket around the cabin all winter. The river still lay under a thick crust of ice several feet thick, snaking a white path through the now green forest.

With the warmer weather and lack of snow we put the skidoo away for the summer and dug Pricey out of hibernation. It took an hour or more of heating her moving bits with a propane flame-thrower called a Tiger torch before she even began to show any vital signs. We felt like Blue Peter presenters waking up the pet tortoise after it'd slept for six months. Once she was awake we were driving into town across the river, which made life a little easier. We could bring more supplies from town, though we still had to walk up to the cabin.

The streets in Dawson were a mud bath. People walked around in wellies with mud stains soaked into their trousers. Trucks and other vehicles looked as if they had just come from an off road contest. This was a sign that break-up wasn't far away, and we had to be prepared for an unknown period of isolation. Once the ice began to rot it would be suicide to try and cross the river. We were making several trips a week to town to buy food and fuel. You could never really tell the state of the ice until you were on top of it, and with each day it became more hazardous.

When the river first breaks, its sides begin to flow, as the ice drops and the surrounding hills release their melt water. You have to drive through a car length of icy water on each side, before you bump onto the main ice in the centre of the river. As the days pass the car length of water becomes deeper and wider until you are driving into a deep, swiftly flowing river with the water coming over the bonnet, under the doors and into the cab through various holes in the rusty floor. The main ice in the centre of the river begins to soften and large holes appear as the constant flow of water erodes the underside.

One particular day we were driving back to the cabin with all sort of necessities including beer. We were onto the main ice when Pricey lurched to one side and stopped - a front tyre had sunk into the ice. We wound down the windows quickly, incase we needed a hasty exit, and sat and waited for a few seconds, bottoms wincing, exchanging concerned glances. I then revved Pricey to the point of no return and let the clutch out. She lurched out of the hole onto solid ice and we took off like an escaped turkey at Christmas until we hit the water on the far bank and burst through it onto solid ground. After that we decided not to cross with the truck. Logic at its best.

Instead we canoed the twenty-yard stretch of open water, climbing out onto the ice, dragging the canoe across to the other side, climbing back in the canoe and paddling to the opposite bank. It was a little hairy getting out of the canoe onto the ice, because it would often break as we climbed out. But being smarter than the average bear (I have an 'O' Level in Art) it didn't take us long to work out that by chipping at the softened ice with an axe first we could be sure of a solid landing.

Bridge had just found a new job with a government programme that dealt with pregnant mums. Because of the isolation here, all pregnant women are considered "at risk" and so are given extra care and attention, a task now entrusted to Bridge. As Bridge was a working girl and me an adventurer on sabbatical we would be separated during break-up. Bridge would stay in town and I would live the bush life with my buddy Boris Lock. It was far easier for Bridge to stay and earn the much needed cash because she had, if required, accommodation with her job and could choose her shifts. We made our final trip into town and I kissed Bridge goodbye on the banks before climbing back into the canoe. We were both very nervous because on the way to town, a large piece of ice the size of a football pitch had broken free next to us with a chilling crack, then floated away. I dragged the canoe onto the main ice and picked my way around the open water with the canoe behind me. I had tied the bowline around my waist and clung to the futile belief that the canoe would be my life line if the ice suddenly went out. It would certainly make my body easier to find. The water was so cold and turbulent, that most people who have fallen in have died from a heart attack before they actually drowned.

Every creak the ice made sent shivers down my spine. I jumped across a wide crack which had just appeared with an amazing boom, hastily put the canoe in the water and paddled to the far bank. I was relieved to be on solid ground once again and waved to a nervous Bridge. That was the last time I would cross until the river was free.

Spring was charging through the forest. You could hear the birds and the jubilant creek, pine martins chased each other through the trees and woodland flowers were pushing their heads out of the frozen ground. The cabin was no longer quiet and still. Squirrels courted and made nests in the roof. The log walls shone golden and bright, creaking occasionally where the sun warmed spots that had been frozen for months. Daylight filtered through the once frozen windows, throwing intricate shadows across the floor.

Things were waking up and on the move. One day a

bull moose scratched its rump on the corner of the cabin, its sheer size blocking the light coming in the windows and its effort literally shaking the cabin. One night I was in the land of nod when Boris let out a throaty growl and climbed into bed with me. I sharply ejected him with my foot but he continued to be on edge, pacing around, growling and sniffing under the door. Something was on the porch raiding my food cache. I sprung out of bed, grabbed a plastic spatula and swaggered to the door. On swinging it open, moonlight reflecting off my 'fair' skin, I stood in total shock as I found myself staring into the hazel, piggy eyes of a big black bear. Its face was smeared with margarine, it had one foot in my food and was sucking on a ham bone as if it was a Henry Winterman's cigar. I called to Boris but he was in my bed, under the covers. The bear blinked, dazzled by my sun-starved body, and fled into the trees like a flying rug. I felt pretty pleased with myself because I had defeated a bear in a way that none of the bronzed northern heroes surrounding me could possibly do.

I would wander through flowers and sunshine to a cliff overlooking the river and Dawson City, where I'd often meet Black Powder Billy, a typical man of the woods. To say he looked a little unhinged was an understatement. He had long, straggly graying hair and beard, carried black powder guns wherever he went, talked as if he was an auctioneer trying to keep up with frantic bidding and swung his arms around as if he had chewing gum on his fingers that he desperately wanted to get rid of. He had little human contact during the winter and had spent many a lonely night listening to CBC radio, which in itself will send a lonely fellow mad. Though a little scary he was a likeable chap and we would spend hours watching the ice and guessing when it would eventually break.

Two weeks after my last trip across the river on a glorious day I was sitting on the look out watching Dawson below. The diesel generator was chugging away supplying the town with power, the general store was taking a delivery of half-dead lettuce and a couple were walking along the riverbank with an enthusiastic dog. A squirrel shot into the tangled branches of the tree beside me as Black Powder Billy came dancing out of the woods waving his gun above his head. "It's breaking, it's breaking!" he shouted, staring wildly up river. I stood up and watched the ice gather speed up the river, taking everything in its path with ground shaking cracks, leaving behind dark clear water. Chunks the size of chest freezers were piling up on each other, and you could hear the ice smash against the rocks and echo down the valley. Submerged icebergs shot skyward in a shower of water as the pressure of the ice moved on. Others would ride up onto a neighbour and flip back into the river, sending a wave of water out across the surrounding ice. The power of the river was incredible.

As soon as the river was free enough I ran to the canoe and paddled into town for a beer and to see Bridge. It hadn't occurred to me that once the main ice on the Yukon had gone, rivers draining into it such as the Stewart River and the White River would quickly free their ice. After about an hour in town I saw great chunks of ice and twisted, broken trees coming down the river. I had to get back quickly because the flow could last for days and Boris was still in the cabin.

I launched the canoe into a small eddy and paddled out into the river. I was not even a third of the way across when the front of the canoe rode up on an iceberg under the water. I frantically back paddled, but I was stuck. I tried to crawl up to the bow and push off but the canoe tipped violently and icy water came over the gunnnel. I fought panic and rocked the canoe backwards and forwards until it shifted slightly and with a lot of hard back paddling I floated free. I could hear Bridge shouting from the bank as another iceberg came out of the water broadside to the canoe and tried its best to tip me over. I couldn't get my paddle into the water, for ice was everywhere. I looked up and saw the cliffs where the ice was crashing at their base loom into sight. If I got caught in the crush on the rocks the canoe would fold in seconds. I panicked, pushing at the ice around me with the paddle. It parted enough to get my paddle in the water and after a lot of desperate strokes I found myself in an eddy just before the bend on the same side of the river I had just left. Bridge came running up, swearing like a dyslexic sailor. It was far too dangerous to cross, Boris would have to wait.

Early the next morning the ice was still flowing but not as much as the day before, so very nervously I pushed the canoe off from the bank and once again paddled into the main current. This time it was a little easier and I eventually made it. I was still further down stream than I wanted to be, but at least I had the right bank. Bridge waved from the far bank as I dragged the canoe to high ground. I was exhausted and shaking and for the first time wished for the easier life we had in Polperro. Once all the ice was gone the government put the ferry back on the river making the journey to town a lot more civilized. It also meant more supplies could reach Dawson, so prices dropped.

June 2000

The Yukon is a mystical place full of legends and history. It is thousands and thousands of miles of untouched wilderness and thankfully the government wants to keep it that way. Probably 60% of its land mass has never felt the tread of human feet, which is wonderful, but which also makes finding a home a little awkward. We had fallen in love with the Yukon and Dawson City and really wanted to put down roots.

We had found a couple of nice areas around Dawson and were applying to the government to lease them, but like anything to do with government it would take ages to complete and would involve a ton of paper work. We could easily have staked a claim and built a cabin somewhere in the territory, but we would never own the land and could only stay if we found gold and worked to recover it. We wanted to build a home we could call our own, and from there venture out into the wilderness on countless adventures in future years.

We were beginning to grow despondent because we couldn't stay in our cabin for long and the government bureaucracy was driving us mad. But then we met an old timer who lived in the woods on top of the hill behind our cabin. Tom was a tall man in his sixties with a silver crew cut, with a face that showed how much he's struggled over the years as well as contempt for his fellow man. It turned out he was tired of the north, and was selling up and moving south. What's more, he was eager to sell.

Bridge and I walked through the woods to the five acres he'd called home for the past ten years. The June sunshine beamed out of the sky onto a breath taking view of the

Tombstone Mountains glowing golden beyond the Klondike valley. A raven whistled, noting our arrival. It was the only sound in the wood that day.

Most of the land was clear of trees, letting in the light and opening the horizon. On one corner stood a small rundown shack that the owner lived in. It was half built and was obviously only supposed to be temporary. All around lay the remnants of abandoned projects that Tom had started with enthusiasm and then given up. The situation and the land were incredibly beautiful but it was marred by a man's negativity and misery. There was no wood shed or food cache. He had simply piled the wood in front of his house and stored food in an old freezer outside his door. He'd given up trying to better his standard of living and just struggled, miserably, through the last few years. It was no wonder he was tired and ready to leave, his spirit had left years ago.

We didn't go into the shack, peering through the dirty windows confirmed our suspicions of its state. But from beneath the remnants of Toms' empty life shone the most amazing promise. I studied Bridge as she wandered around, feeling its potential. A broad grin decorated her pretty face and a sparkle twinkled within her deep brown eyes. She looked like a long lost child who had come home. It was obvious our search was over. The next adventure had begun.

Part II

September 20th

Up here summer turns to winter very quickly. One minute it's July, the sun is shining for 24 hours a day, everybody is full of energy and huge moose steaks are being roasted on barbecues. The next it's September, it's getting dark at about 8 p.m., skiffs of ice start forming on water buckets and it's pretty cold inside our sleeping bags and we're definitely not ready for it. In England in September you go to Blackpool and dip your toe in the sea, eat ice creams and buy crab sticks from a man in a dirty blue-and-white-stripped apron. The last thing on your Bank Holiday mind is a white bloody Christmas.

September 21st

We are toasting marshmallows on the embers of the rambled shack that used to stand on our land when a movement catches Bridge's eye. "What was that?" she whispers to me as she pulls her wool blanket closer round her shoulders. I look through the glow of the fire and see nothing but the dark spruce silhouetted against a cloud-covered sky. "Your imagination," I say, and return to retrieving my marshmallow from a piece of smoldering wood. "It's snow!" she shouts a couple of minutes later. "It's snowing, look!" And there they are, snowflakes the size of squished sheep spiralling down from heavy clouds. It is a shock. To us, it is still ice cream and crabs sticks time.

We lie that night in our sleeping bags and there's not a sound outside the tent except for the gentle whisper of snow falling on the canvas above our heads.

September 22nd

We have awoken to a beautiful white world. Snow is two inches deep on everything from the smallest spruce needle to the embers of the odd two by four that had missed being ceremoniously burnt last night. The trouble with all this beauty and whiteness is that we've burnt the shack, and our only protection is the small canvas tent I made on my arrival in Canada. Which is now sagging from the weight of snow. "Right!" says Bridge, "we need a structure, any structure will do!" I take my cue.

With my chainsaw I trudge through the silent forests looking for suitable trees. I find one quickly and pull the chainsaw's start cord with all the flair of a true blue Canadian lumber jack. Then I pull the cord again, then again, and again until perspiration pours from my wrinkled, red brow into the frozen snow beneath my feet. "Never fear! Who dares wins," I say to the ravens, as I take out my trendy pocket Leatherman, a tool which no sensible or sober northern hero should ever be without. I hunt for something called a spark plug and unscrew anything that my Leatherman seems to fit. Half an hour later, surrounded by orange casings, oily nuts and with a bolt freezing to my numb fingers I let out the traditional northern call of the wild. "What the **** am I ******* doing in a ******* stupid god forsaken ******* place like this **** hole!"

September 24th

Snow falls in a constant flow from an overcast, low-lying sky. Everything is silent and in hiding. Bridge has gone for a walk with Boris because he was getting very nervous with each increasingly imaginative curse I shrieked as I tried in vain to put back together my chainsaw in the warmth of the tent.

September 26th

I finally have the chainsaw back together, though it runs like a drug-crazed rapper with a sore throat. I'm a bit concerned about the amount of blue smoke and backfiring it's doing, which might be something to do with the three small screws I have left over.

I am taken aback by the power and ruthlessness of the tool in my hand. I actually managed to fell a tree this afternoon. After a few seconds of twiddling my thumb in a haze of blue smoke I sent a magnificent tree crashing earthward, smashing down many smaller trees with it. The tree had been growing for 400 years, giving life to countless wildlife. For the first time in my life I realised the impact that man, our arrogance and our tools can have on this amazing and fragile world we are lucky enough to live in for a brief moment.

Once quiet had returned to the forest, I was filled with an amazing feeling of power and satisfaction. This was better than any computer game I had ever played. I could destroy whole ecosystems to build my outhouse. I could devastate a complete crossbill breeding area to create my sitting room. I could even destroy permafrost containing ancient mammoth poop and alter the vegetation on the forest floor, just so I could open a carton of orange juice on a flat surface in a swanky kitchen.

With the sort of deranged smile only seen on moonlit nights in deserted graveyards, I trudged through the snow felling suitable trees to make the foundations of our castle. Cutting them down was one thing but cleaning them, cutting them into the right lengths and dragging them back to the cabin was an entirely different matter. Even after I had dismembered them and cut them to eight foot lengths, the trees were as heavy as a British Rail bacon and lettuce sandwich. I staggered for hours dragging them up the 100 foot hill out of a valley, through the snow and down hill 300 yards to our land. Back at camp I'd flop into the snow with another chunk of tree and Bridge would leave her job of peeling bark and help lift me up, turn me around and send me back staggering into the forest.

October 1st

At last we have enough relatively straight and peeled logs for the foundation of a cabin. The only problem is, I know nothing about building houses. The only one I ever built was several years ago, and that was out of Lego. I remember it stood up rather well, until my brother threw his Stretch Armstrong at it.

We decide it's time to do some research. The town bookshop is full of all sorts of useful books about building birdhouses and other garden furniture, the art of plumbing in a kitchen sink and the many ways to 'play with plywood'. When we enquire about building log cabins, a bubbly girl with a fantastic smile directs us to a low shelf full of dusty books. There's 'Holistic Medicine', '101 Things to do With Hemp', 'Survival in the Forest' and, of course, 'How to build a Log Cabin' by a skinny little man called Don Pilgrim. I flick through it briefly and buy it because of a sentence I have never been able to find since. 'Keep your cabin simple and rustic'. I could easily do that.

During the longer evenings I bore Bridge and Boris with the book. Pilgrim seems to start building his log cabin with a lovely supply of straight, uniform, peeled and dried logs neatly stacked on site. He doesn't seem to have to drag long pieces of lumber back home then spend six hours a day in temperatures of -10°C peeling them with a draw knife. And there's not even a mention of how pine sap get everywhere and warms up in your tent at night, glues your hair together and sticks to your clothes and skin like super glue.

Each night brings a more crisp and chilling cold, drawing us out into the silver frozen wilds, which look truly magical. There is total stillness, the northern lights ripple through the sky, arching from mountain to mountain, and the crunchy snow reflects every light from the stars to the hiding moon.

October 3rd

Bridge gets up well before light. She is meeting a friend on the road to go shopping - or rather, moose hunting. I begin to dig a hole for a new outhouse, a really deep hole this time, and am getting rather tired of digging when Bridge and Sandy come through the trees grinning widely. "We've got a moose," Bridge says excitedly. I leap out of my two-foot hole and ask to see it, but the 700lb dead moose is still in the bush and I am needed to help get it out. This is going to be a long day.

The extreme effort it takes to retrieve a dead moose from the bush is a way of earning your meat. We find ours in a clump of willows next to a rapidly freezing stream. It's lying on its stomach with its long legs tucked underneath, as if it's having a little sleep. Its head alone is over three feet long. After much deliberation about what exactly to do, we all grab the only leg we can reach and struggle to roll the moose over. As we do so another leg springs out, narrowly missing Sandy's head. I instruct the ladies to hold onto the back leg while I unleash my bowie knife and try to gut the huge belly. The skin is so tough I can't get the knife passed the fur.

After several violent stabs a vale of steam erupts into the air and the guts spill onto the snow. Hours later we have the moose cut into pieces four legs, ribs, neck, haunches and head. We have at least 500lbs of meat that would feed us for a year. Sandy's truck is about two miles away and I have to carry each enormous piece of moose over some amazingly awkward terrain. The effort is incredible. With the help of the ladies I hoist a leg at a time onto my shoulder and stumble through the bush for 50 yards, then collapse in exhaustion.

It is dark by the time we have all the meat hanging from a pole tied high between two trees next to our camp. The moose's fur is incrusted with snow and the shine of life in its eyes has finally dimmed to opaque. We stand in silence, thanking the animal for giving itself to us. It's a very humbling experience, hunting and killing such an amazing animal. In one way the relief of getting meat before winter is overwhelming but in another, the sorrow for the animal is sickening. I don't think we will ever get used to it - not that we should.

October 4th

Something was sniffing around the hanging moose in the night. There are some very large (dog?) prints in the snow and we heard wolves howling yesterday, though they were a long way off. I am going to hang the meat further away from camp today.

October 7th

I've got the foundation finished for the cabin, it looks small but I suppose we can add to it when and if little ones arrive. Bridge has started work in town, once again looking after Dawson's mums. We will need money to get winter supplies and I need to buy some wood-working tools - the chainsaw is very unreliable and doesn't seem to cut anything straight.

October 9th

The pressure of freeze up is on. Ice is running down the river in chunks the size of small cars, colliding into the ferry that is still trying to keep the route to Alaska joined with Dawson. The shore ice is creeping further into the river, narrowing the passage for the bergs. If these cold nights continue the ice will be too thick for the ferry, the government will pull it from the water and the river will be impassable, even in a canoe. We have to prepare for at least a month of being cut off. Bridge is going to keep working in town during Freeze Up, which gives me enough time to build some sort of cabin without having to do washing up or waste time cleaning up after myself.

Today I visited a chap I've heard of who mills logs. Boris and I drove Pricey into a snow-covered yard outside of town. Lumber of every dimension was piled high in all directions. I parked next to a big wooden shed with the words 'don't think, lift' painted in a less than vertical line above the door. I swung open the heavy 12 foot doors and was hit by a blast of heat from a barrel stove in a corner. "Shut the freaken door!" bellowed a man at least 50 feet tall, dressed in a blood-stained blue overall and holding a seven inch knife dripping with blood. "What do you want?" he said, splattering blood on my new lumber jack shirt which I had bought to wear when dealing in trees. It was then I saw a half-butchered moose hanging in the back.

This was Hinze, and he loved to talk wood. He showed me with enthusiasm various cuts of wood in different widths and thickness. There was only spruce, because that's all that grows here, but it was already cut to length, so I bought as much as I could fit into Pricey.

October 14th

They pulled the ferry from the ice today. I watched from the west bank with a sort of morbid interest until the town lights were switched on, then hiked back up through the woods contemplating when I might next use a porcelain toilet or see my wife. It might be weeks, it could be months. All I know is that I am going to have a cabin for Bridget by he time she can cross.

It is completely dark by the time I reach the lumber pile I bought from Hinze. Standing in total silence with nothing but snow covered trees around me it dawns on me that I am stuck here with Boris and it is impossible to get to the only town in 600 miles. It takes a couple of Hollywood style slaps across the face to become accustomed to my situation. What's a couple of months without seeing anyone and having no comforts? I just hope my chainsaw stays friendly and refrains from chewing into my leg.

It's a strange feeling sitting alone in the tent tonight. The only light is from a flickering candle that keeps going out whenever a chilly breeze flaps the door. I am totally alone, for the first time in a very long time. I can't remember ever feeling this alone. Boris is here but he's hardly eloquent enough to have a decent conversation with, without the stimulus of a very large bottle of whisky.

People somewhere are cramming onto tube trains, fighting for a little bit of dignified personal space. Others are trying to meet deadlines, or lying awake worrying about their mounting debts, middle age spread or a major world crises that I am not even aware of. Some people are having a party, enjoying themselves, flirting with the hosts' blonde sister with the sexy legs. It all seems so far away from me here, especially the hosts' sister with the sexy legs.

The stove is crackling away in the corner, the wolves are howling across the valley. I must have stood outside the tent for at least an hour and soaked up the lonesomeness. There is a certain amount of fear that I really need to hold at bay. I am totally responsible for my well being and I'm using a chainsaw in the morning. If I cut my leg even slightly I am immediately in a very dangerous, perhaps life-threatening situation. No one will pass by or come up to visit for cucumber sandwiches and a cup of tea. If I am lucky, Brent, my closest neighbour, might decide he needed a hand from an Englishman who, whenever he lifts anything remotely heavy, grimaces worse than Mick Jaggar in the middle of 'Angie'.

This was nothing like the break up I had experienced last spring. Back then loneliness was not a factor, life all around me was awakening whether from a butterfly, song bird or flower. Then it was only a matter of time before the ice broke. Now it is about everything dying, leaving or hunkering down for a long miserable winter.

October 16th

I am extremely cold this morning. A strong north wind gathered strength in the night and whistled under the tent, howling worse than the distant wolves. I decide to cut spruce bows to line the floor of the tent. They are supposed to insulate the frozen ground and right now every little bit counts.

As I walk through the woods I think about building a wall. I have no plans or designs, only a few bits of tree and some milled lumber of various dimensions somewhere under the snow. It's a daunting prospect, and I wish Bridge were here to discuss it with.

Later I retire to the tent. I have no idea what the time is but it's been dark about an hour, which would put it at about 5.00 p.m. The spruce bows on the floor of the tent smell strongly of pine, which reminds me of Christmas. The fire is still crackling away in the corner and I've bought a whole heap of wood in, so it should last the night.

I am curled up in my sleeping bag, trying to digest a hunk of moose meat, when I notice the odd stray spark fly out of the stove and settle on the spruce bows. The bows begin to smoulder. I jump to my feet and stamp out the offending sparks, creating my own little Fred Astaire dance routine. After doing the same thing five times I realise these sparks had simply fizzled out on the frozen floor of the tent before.

To put my mind at rest, I invent a sort a back country smoke alarm. I put Boris's bed right in front of the stove, which he thinks is high praise indeed, until the first spark lands in his fur. He springs up and howls, trailing smoke and fireworks, consequently waking me up to administer the necessary steps to avert a tent fire.

October 17th

I awake when it is still dark and begin the daunting task of building a wall. I've given up on my chainsaw for the time being, and instead am using my new circular saw that plugs into a tiny generator bought for such a purpose. I'm not too sure which is quicker because the generator takes a long time to coax into action. The problem this morning is the amount of ice in the carburettor. If I didn't know about mechanics before coming to the Yukon, I'm going to have a diploma in it by the time freeze up is over. The wall looks sort of upright and seems to do the job of being a wall. But looking at it again, I think I should have put a window in.

October 18th

I am quickly settling down to the fact that it is dark from 5:00 p.m. to 9:00 a.m. and I need to build for 12 hours a day just to get a roof over our heads by the end of the month. Maybe then I'll be able to get some real heat, and be able to thaw out my left big toe that left for market weeks ago and isn't the slightest bit interested in 'wee weeing' it all the way home.

Last night the temperature was probably around 20 below. The stove in the tent keeps the chill off but the spruce bows don't stop the cold coming up through the ground and chewing into my kidneys. I have to keep rolling like a lump of dead animal on a spit to keep warm. The worst thing is getting out of bed, because my sleeping bag isn't perfect for winter camping. I go to bed in everything I own including old socks retrieved from Bridge's ragbag. Consequently it makes it impossible to shed the sleeping bag each morning and get warm.

But being the adventurer that I am I have developed a morning routine. Instead of staggering sleepily into a warm shower then wandering around in my dressing gown sipping coffee and eating Marmite on toast, I strip to my Y-fronts, expose my body to the crisp morning air and watch it contract to look like a greedy corn fed turkey that has been plucked by a drunk with four broken fingers. I then throw on all my clothes again and surprisingly enough begin to feel the rather unusual sensation of relative comfort returning to my bones. I then dare to get the fire going and roast a frozen unrecognisable part of a moose on a green stick with the hope, often in vain, of eating it without having to retrieve it from the flames with ash stuck to it and the loss of my eyebrows. Then, and only then, do I venture into the unknown world of Mr. Pilgrim.

The problem is that it is still dark and will be for quite some time. I know it's morning somewhere in the world but that is about it. With no clock, a cold bed and a job to do who knows what time I awake. All I know is that I need light. Being without electricity for over a year now is my only excuse as to why I forgot to buy a light to plug into the generator. After a week staggering around in the dark tripping over lumber, the chainsaw, the dog, the guy ropes and the odd frozen sock I've forgot to put back on during my morning ritual, I've decided I have to go on a quest for light.

After an hour of searching a creek in the dark I find my trusty steed (the skidoo) where I had left it last spring. I scrape the snow from her and lift the bonnet. Everything to my unskilled eye seems to still be there. The only thing missing is part of the seat, which a bear has eaten. I jump on and pull the start cord. Nothing happens. I fiddle around with the spark plug for a while and, being a true bushman, pee on the carburettors to defrost them. The next time I pull the cord a faint flickering light undulates across the snow in front to me. With some gentle nurturing of the throttle the machine shakes into life and the headlight intensifies, picking up the bright eyes of Boris as he bounces around, barking with excitement that the skidoo is actually running. He knows we are going somewhere and he doesn't care where, so long as he can chase. I rev the engine and hold my breath as the usual rank blue smoke spews out and does its best to choke me. Then with a roar we take off into the night. Or morning.

I follow a trail through the spruce and then hit the Top of the World Highway, which has not seen traffic for a very long time judging by the deep pristine snow that sprays over the windscreen of the skidoo as I charge through it. I then cut back into the forest and follow the dog trail into Brent's yard.

His dog team make such a racket on our arrival that I quickly see the strike of a match inside his cabin, then the glow of a Kerosene lamp being carried to the door. A blurry-eyed Brent stands in a pair of bright red long johns, shouts at his dogs who immediately fall silent, then drops his awakening gaze to me. He is still for a moment, then holds the kerosene lamp aloft and says: "What the hell are you doing tearing around on a misfiring skidoo at 3.00 a.m. in the morning with that mad short legged dog chasing you?"

After initial sarcasm at my request Brent offers me a 1960s lava lamp which he's never used. I find it sitting on a bale of straw covered in 30 years of dust. It looks more like a hog turd in a jar of acid but it's a light, so I take it. Back at my log pile I start the generator and plug in the lamp, eager to get building another wall. Moments later a strange purple glow emanates from the light and lumps of purple goo start moving about inside in a strangely fascinating style.

With light I have action. My only dilemma is the fact that whenever I start my electrical saw the generator coughs and slows, the lava lamp dims almost to a glow and I am left guessing where my perfectly straight cut on the wood is. Only when my cutting is over does the generator pick up and the lava lamp brighten, showing my delicate cut to be somewhere between Bognor Regis and the Isle of Skye.

October 19th

Last night another heavy snowfall buried all the lumber again. I have discovered I don't have a spirit level so I'm using a glass of water, which I have to watch because it freezes pretty quickly. If I'm not careful the cabin will have more of a lean to it than a wino outside an off-license. I haven't seen Boris for a day or two. The last time I saw him was down at the river, I do hope he has enough brains not to try and cross no matter how bushed he's getting.

October 21st

With two walls up and joined together in the corner I took the day off to check out the river and to see if I could find Boris. I took my gun in the hope of seeing a poor, hapless grouse or a rabbit which would have given my poor teeth a rest from the tough moose. But I didn't have any luck. The sunset is incredible this evening. Only a few of the endless spruce covered hills are touched with its golden light, spreading soft colour onto the snow and the otherwise black and white world. I am sitting below a huge spruce - it has no snow below its sheltered branches, so I come here quite a lot. As I write the golden light is turning in seconds to a light red and a huge full moon is touching the mountains in front of me. It reflects the golden colour of the sun, and as it climbs into the rapidly darkening sky it takes on its distinct white shine. I feel I can almost touch it.

The woods around me are now in complete darkness but the snow is crystal white from the huge moon, giving me a spotlighted trail to take me back to the solitude of my tent.

My tent feels like a tardis. It looks so small now the snow is covering it but inside it's a world, my world. No matter how minimal, the warmth hits you as soon as you duck under the door flap. The stove sings to me - it pops, crackles and snorts, like a friendly dependable dog.

October 24th

Boris came back today. I think he's been gone a few days, but I'm losing track of time. He is limping badly on his front leg and he has ice encrusted inches-deep into his fur. His testicles have at least two inches of ice around them and he is exhausted. I've brought him into the tent and stoked up the stove. He's trying to bite the ice from his privates as his back steams but I'm trying to stop him because he is drawing blood.

With the lava lamp bubbling away I got an early start this morning. I now have three walls up, though they definitely don't look square and upright. I'm hoping I can square everything up when the fourth wall is in place. The weather has warmed to -5°C and a light freezing rain has been falling all morning, making my already monumental task more difficult. A layer of ice now covers everything. My hammer was frozen to the floor this morning and it's difficult to get the wood to fit properly with an inch of ice between the join, no matter how hard I cuss. The ice on the beams also means that my trusty level doesn't sit flat. If it was difficult to get anything level with a half-frozen cup of water before, now it's virtually impossible.

My morale is low. I've hit my thumb twice, once really hard and now the cold is making it very painful. I hold it out at an odd angle to protect it but this seems to make it worse as it is constantly getting knocked against all manner of solid objects. I took my glove off to have a look and it looks more like the filling of a frozen blueberry pie than a thumb. I wonder if it is broken?

October 25th

I had an excellent surprise today. I was about to stop work when I heard a helicopter approaching. It took awhile to see it, looking extremely small against the backdrop of mountains and spruce valleys. It circled the camp and then landed in a hale of snow and a wind that nearly knocked my castle over. I was amazed to see Bridge jump out and run clear of the blades, holding down her fur hat with one hand and carrying a bottle of wine in the other. I waved to the pilot who winked at me, made a rude gesture with his forearm, then lifted back into the air and disappeared behind the trees.

Silence returned to the camp as I looked at Bridge in sheer amazement. Apparently, the pilot was on a supply run down the river and Bridge had hitched a ride. He'll be back in the morning to pick her up. I knew I should have done the washing up.

October 26th

I'm on cloud nine this morning. I've even had a wash and a shave and my thumb is trusted up like a wounded soldier. Boris has had his balls smeared with antiseptic cream (Bridge is so brave, I had refused to touch the rancid things) and is radiating with the love Bridge has showed him. The helicopter returned as promised to pick Bridge up, and they have just disappeared behind the mountains.

We had a very romantic night last night chewing chunks of moose under the northern lights and drinking a well overdue bottle of wine. It was heaven. Bridge loved the cabin, if that's what you can call it, she thinks it a little small but agrees we can always add on when little ones arrive. After talking it over with her I now know where to put the windows, the kitchen and maybe one-day the bathroom. She really is a breath of fresh air wherever she goes. I forget how refreshing she is to have around, how level headed and sensible. Nothing is a problem to her, everything is exciting and a delight. She is so full of life and love and so willing to share it.

I spent most of the daylight hours cutting firewood. I'm getting more skilled at cutting lumber to the right length, so the off cuts and mistakes that have been keeping us warm quite nicely until now are in short supply, and the stove does take a lot of feeding.

I saw the river again today and there seems to be no stopping the ice flow. Town is only a half a mile away when you're standing on the west bank of the river, but it might as well be in China.

October 29th (I Think)

Today I moved out of the tent and into the cabin. I've transplanted the stove into one corner of the cabin and tarped in the roof. Tonight Boris and I are having a disco to celebrate! The lava lamp is doing some amazing, purple shadow work on the walls and the generator is popping and gyrating very tunefully. I'm the disc jockey and I've put on my woolly hat and sunglasses to look the part. I control the beat (yeah man!) by twiddling the throttle on the electric saw. Everything goes dark and Boris and I dance.

Poor Boris is a crap dancer. I stomp around the cabin nodding my head like a swimming coot and twiddling the trigger on the saw to my advantage. After doing some energetic barking and twirling that only he understands, Boris has given up and is sulking next to the stove. I'm enjoying the luxury of the generator for probably the last time because my petrol situation is very low and I want to save what is in the skidoo for emergencies.

I am getting very tired of moose meat although I am very grateful for it. I ran out of store-bought food a while ago including bread, eggs, bacon, even coffee, though I thought we had enough for a month. Maybe it's not October any more? I'm also running out of candles. Soon I will be totally restricted to the Yukon's wishes and that's sleep for 19 hours and work for five.

October ?th

The strangest thing happened today. I was standing in the snow in total silence and feeling unbelievably alone when a little bird somewhere in the woods started to sing a lovely warbling song that literally warmed the air around me. It's nice to know I'm not the only thing alive in this black and white world.

There is a wind in the air that is whispering warnings, of what I don't know, but I'm sure I'll find out.

Two Days Later

Ouch! The temperature feels as if it has dropped out of the bottom of the thermometer. The crystal clear skies are always an omen that something's going to happen. I felt the cold seeping into the cabin like the rising tide last night. It was unstoppable. No matter how much I stuffed the stove it could not keep the chill out. I had to yell at Boris at one point because he was burning the hair on his back by lying too close to the stove. I awoke to frost all over my sleeping bag. My breath condensed as soon as it hit the cabin air. I couldn't see it because I had pulled the hood of my sleeping bag up over my face and only had an air hole the size of a wine cork to breathe through. I lifted the piece of frozen canvas covering the door to see a two-inch layer of feathery frost and feel a blast of 40 below air. It was like accidentally inhaling snuff.

Stupidly I decided that the 'chilly weather' wasn't going to stop me putting up my roof. After all, I had all the logs peeled and ready. I dressed in everything I owned and stuffed my jacket pocket with nails and a hammer, then unstuck the ridge beam from the ground with a few hefty swings of a sledgehammer. I couldn't lift the whole thing at once but managed to drag one end up the makeshift scaffolding, which consisted of the frozen moose head, various piles of firewood, the skidoo and two planks of various thickness.

After a lot of grunting and farting I had the ridge beam in place. The trouble was keeping it there. I was at full stretch with both hands on the end of the beam, my face pressed firmly against my scaffolding (which was too close to the wall) and a 40 below draft whistling up my back because my jacket had ridden up. I needed to get one nail in to hold the beam in place. I fumbled for my nails and pulled out six at once from my bulging pocket, but I couldn't get my hammer out of the other pocket because I was holding the nails with one hand and the beam with the other. I put the nails in my mouth, grabbed the hammer and managed to transfer it into the hand holding the ridge beam. Then I tried to retrieve a nail from my mouth. All six of them were stuck firmly to my lip. I swore and the nails then became stuck to the tip of my tongue. I tried to pull them from my mouth but it was incredibly painful.

I pondered my situation as the cold crept over my exhausted body. I was standing on tiptoes on a frozen moose head with 40 below air flowing up my back. My hand holding the hammer was becoming so cold and numb I was expecting to feel the hammer bounce onto my cranium any minute and I was drooling worse than Boris waiting to be fed. The drool was freezing instantly into my beard and hanging in two icicles that were on a fast track down my neck. My beard was frozen to my jacket collar so I had to keep my neck tilted to avoid ripping my beard out. This was probably not the smartest thing I had ever done.

It was when the hammer fell from my frozen fingers and hit me on the head, pulling the bobble hat clean off my head, that I let go of the ridge beam and jumped clear of the scaffolding. I slipped on an off cut of 2x4 and rolled into a snow bank headfirst. My eyes were shut but I could hear the devastation the ridgepole was doing to my walls as it smashed earthwards. It's very hard to move when you're wearing everything you own but I rolled around in the snow bank and finally became vertical. My mouth was full of snow because my bottom lip was sagging so much with the weight of six 3-inch nails stuck to it. My teeth thought I was eating really cold ice cream and a powerful headache arched across my skull. I was exhausted. The 40 below air was sapping my strength, burning my ears and freezing the snow I was covered in onto my skin.

I wanted to lie down in the snow and give up, not to be

discovered until someone drove into the yard and punctured their tyres on my mouth. It was then that Brent appeared out of nowhere on his dog sled. "It's 45 below for Christ sake," Brent said, looking at me very strangely. I stood up and said "Ugggghhhhhh." His dogs, obviously scared out of their wits, took off into the trees. Brent gave chase, yelling all manner of obscenities about the English, and returned five minutes later with his quivering dogs. "That got me sweating," he said, "I hate sweating at 45 below."

Once Brent had stoked the stove to the hilt, boiled some water and released me from the six nails he said, "Congratulations, you're going to be a father." I wanted to say "What?" but only managed a pathetic "Uh?" because my tongue was swollen worse than a two-week dead toad. Bridget had called him on the bush phone and asked him to relay the message.

Brent has just left, my tongue is extremely sore and I have no skin on the inside of my bottom lip. I always thought the moment I found out we were going to have a baby would be perfect. Bridge would one day come home from a sneaky trip to the doctors with a radiant glow. I would ask her if she was alright and she would smile and say something like, "I've never been better. We're going to have a baby." I would then hug her jubilantly and lay my hand on her stomach in a protecting manner. Bridge would say, "Oh, don't be silly, I'm alright", then go to the fridge and make strawberry jam and pickled herring sandwiches with a side dressing of gherkins.

I never dreamt in my widest nightmares that I would be looking like a frosted garden rake when I heard the news, or that I would not be able to hold Bridge in my arms. That's the worst thing of all. I can't even see her. See if she is alright, see if she has everything she needs or if she is eating a strawberry jam and pickled herring sandwich with a side dressing of gherkins. What can I do?

The Next Day (Probably Nov 2nd)

I'm pacing like a caged tiger. I've just come back from the river, which is still flowing and shows no sign of stopping. You can't see the water, just huge, round plates of thick, white ice spinning in the current. I went to see Brent to ask if I could use his bush phone to call Bridge, but apparently she is staying in a cabin on the gold creeks with no power or phone. I really need to talk to her, to see if she and the baby are alright. I can't work on the house. I can't do anything.

This morning I went for a walk to try and shoot a grouse. I had one in my sight but got a pang of guilt - maybe this creature was somebody's son, or even worse, somebody's mother whose babies needed her. Why the hell didn't it fly for cover? It was just standing there waiting and watching with little black beady eyes. In the end I threw a snowball at it and, after a little thought, it flew into the trees.

November 3rd

The temperature is still somewhere below -40°C. I've managed to patch the walls back together - luckily the ridgepole didn't do as much damage as I first thought but now I can't bear to be inside. This cabin I was so proud of making has suddenly become a silly game and I keep expecting Stretch Armstrong to come falling through the roof accompanied by my brother's asthmatic laugh. I think I'm getting cabin fever. I'll take two of my headache pills and see what happens.

November 4th

I had a brain wave in the middle of the night. There is an old aluminium boat down by the river. If I cut a hole in it, mount my skidoo on the back and skim across the flowing ice to town I could hold my family in my arms! Brilliant. I don't need to be able to steer, all I have to do is hit the far bank somewhere and walk to town. I don't know why I didn't think of it earlier instead of eating half a bottle of headache tablets.

Just as it is getting light I find the old boat and break it free of the frozen ground. I fire up my chain saw and cut a big hole in the back, large enough for my skidoo track to fit in. I've just finished when Brent arrives, looking at me even stranger than usual. "What the hell are you doing to my boat?" he says in a less than civil manner. "Your boat?" I say. I apologise profusely and feel like a teenager caught defacing the school bike shed, but then I enthusiastically explain my real urge to get to town. No one was going to stop me, not even him, and I was so self-righteous and confident I even surprised myself.

Brent calmly brings me back to reality. "You're a stupid idiot, what good is an unborn without a father?" Dying was not something I'd contemplated while I hacked out the back of his boat. All of a sudden taking risks and being adventurous has a new set of consequences. Common sense prevailed, but I'm sitting here still filled with longing.

November 11th

I'm trying to keep busy. Brent came up today and helped me put the roof system on the cabin. The weather has warmed up to 25 below so things went a little more smoothly. It makes such a difference having another pair of hands and Brent, I found out, is remarkably patient. There is a bright moon out tonight and it's casting a silver light over the tortured land. I don't need the lava lamp or candles to read my very old and tattered National Geographic. Next year I'm going to do what everybody else does and rent 20 to 30 trashy novels from the library for three months. My thumb is getting better and I'm beginning to get my taste back, though this is in some ways a hindrance because I cook as well as Rambo reads poetry.

November 24th

Well, I have a cabin sealed to the weather. We have no windows yet but the holes in the wall are covered by plastic. Having a roof makes a huge difference to the temperature in here, though now the hard part is finished I'm finding it difficult to concentrate on the interior. I haven't heard a thing from Bridge since Brent relayed the message some time ago. I keep wondering whether she is feeling sick in the mornings or if she has a little bump yet. But always on the back of my mind is how she will cope in this small, dark, cold cabin. We are going to have to work out some better way of getting water. Melting snow is all right but we have to get a lot of snow for a cup of water and the melting pot is far too heavy for a pregnant lady to be carrying in and out of the cabin.

November 26th

Hurrah! I checked the river today and it looks like the ice has jammed just south of the town before the mouth of the Klondike River. Boris and I were up at the lookout for a least an hour watching it. The jam is probably 200 feet in length and stretches from bank to bank. The flowing ice is bashing into it and some is being forced underneath, only to reappear minutes later in broken chunks down river. I could hear the grinding and breaking of the bergs a good mile away.

I'm feeling pretty confident I can cross the Yukon and I'm going to try in the morning. The Klondike may be more difficult, but there is a bridge across it two miles upstream, I can always walk to that.

November 27th

I pack my rucksack with an axe, a change of clothes, some matches, dry fire starter and a hunk of cooked moose meat, then drive on the skidoo to the jammed section. I'm hoping I'll be able to skidoo right across in one short burst of two stroke power, but once down on the river bank I see that's impossible. Huge icebergs are condensed together and large open patches of dark steaming water lie everywhere. The rumble of bergs being pushed underneath and breaking up is all very unnerving. I think about turning round and waiting for a couple of days to make sure the jam will hold but the urge to see Bridge overrides reason.

With my heart in my mouth, my axe at the ready and a very long pole locked horizontally between my forearms and chest, I venture onto the ice. I haven't gone 50 feet when I hear a loud crack, and patch of ice ahead of me, probably 30 feet square, moves enough for the recent snow covering it to fall into the big cracks that appeared out of nowhere. I wait with my right knee doing the Saturday Night Fever and fear making me sing 'Onward Christian Soldiers' in a very shaky six year old's voice. Nothing else happens, so I gingerly carry on, moving very slowly and very, very carefully.

Before I know it I am out in the middle of the river, the safety of the spruce-covered banks a long way off. I climb over a heap of bergs and meet a wide patch of dark, thin ice, which hours ago was a steaming pool of water. I look for a way around but there isn't one. I am surrounded by almost vertical bergs on one side and open, steaming, hissing water on the other. I sit on the top of the ice for a while to decide what to do.

The ice is continually cracking and moving. I am already a good two thirds of the way across but it's very difficult to tell the thickness of ice. I pull my axe from my pack and while standing on a berg wearily hit the black ice in front of me. Nothing happens, so I hit harder, and after three or four blows with the axe I break through, but only slightly. The ice is probably about four inches thick. Is it strong enough to walk on? My mind goes back to the puddles England's roads. Some were only an inch or so deep but when they froze you could walk on them. There's a very strong current continually wearing the ice here but I was sure the ice could take my weight.

I grasp my pole like a long lost lover and step out onto the black ice. Every step I take is nerve-racking. I can see through the thin ice into the very dark and endless water rushing below. It is very scary. Under my feet is a gateway between life and death and I don't trust it. I should not be out here! My knees shake and my breathing quickens. The steam rising from the open water makes a fog and I have to try really hard to keep my direction. At one point the turbulent water is above the actual ice I'm walking on, rising in turmoil before giving way to the ice and ducking under. I think about turning back several times but I cannot describe the feeling I have to hold Bridget in my arms. It is as if she is draining my mental energy and the only way I can recharge is to dock into her arms. I reach the bergs on the other side of the black ice and collapse into a shaking heap. I'm sure I can see my heart beating out of my neck and the adrenaline making me glow neon. The relief to get onto white solid ice again is incredible.

I sit shaking and looking at the black ice for a long time. It has my faint footprints on it now, but tomorrow it could be gone. I feel truly alive. I'm putting myself through situations I would only have dreamt about in Polperro. I literally vibrate with excitement. But after my adrenaline calms, the big picture becomes clear again. I've always thought my motto to be 'I'll have a pint please,' but after that crossing it's definitely, 'My wife before my life'.

When I reach the far bank the feeling of being on solid ground is quite overwhelming. I am now on the side of my family. They are walking on this same ground. I trudge up through the trees and along the bank of the Klondike. After about 40 minutes of looking for a place to cross I resign myself to the fact that I will have to walk to the bridge and then back into town.

As I reach Dawson I am amazed to see Christmas lights draped haphazardly around windows and along balconies. It's a little early, I think, but it is very welcoming. I head for the nearest bar and order a cheeseburger and a glass of beer.

The barman greets me with enthusiasm. "Dorian! You made it across the river. Nice beard... Jeez, you look thin."

The same old regulars are in there, watching the river on the local TV station as the camera pans backwards and forwards on a remote pole, broadcasting a continual picture. One of them coughs as if he is gasping his last breath, then lights a cigarette with a shaking hand, another rubs the front of his woolly hat as if he has an unwanted lodger beneath it, another sits motionless and far away. I ask them if anyone has seen Bridget. They suddenly became animated and all reply in unison, as if I'd put a quarter in a box to spark them into life. "Yeah, she's pregnant you know. Boy you look thin. Merry Christmas!" Just then my burger arrives, topped with fresh lettuce leaves and tomato. I haven't had anything like them for a very long time and they taste incredible.

After my burger I walk down Main Street. The few people who are around are busy loading their trucks with huge amounts of groceries, liquor and fluffy toys. People greet me with, "Hey Dorian, you made it to town... Boy you look thin... Bridge's pregnant... Merry Christmas."

It is when I go to get the post that I finally see Bridge. She is wearing a fur hat, a Parka four sizes too big for her and a glow I've never seen before. I watch her through the window of the post office talking enthusiastically to the vicar. She keeps sweeping her long black hair behind her ear and tapping the top of her hat. She laughs, exposing white teeth and sheer lust for life.

I wait for her to come outside. I leant nonchalantly on the handrail of the steps, readjusting my position several times. I lick my fingers and try to flatten hair that hasn't seen a brush for weeks. I practise what I will say. "Hey, Babe how's it going," or maybe, "in all the post offices in all the world you had to walk into mine." I even practise the way I hold my mouth. Should I have a slight leer, a smile or a cool nonchalant look? I am in the process of practising a 'you looking for me?' leer when she comes out. She stops dead in her tracks at the top of the steps and says "Dorian! Are you drunk?" The vicar gives me a funny look, I feel two inches tall and give up looking cool. I stand up to say the usual "hi" when Bridge leaps off the top steps into my arms.

It is only after a cup of coffee with Bridge that I find out it is December the 19th, and that the whole town knows she's pregnant. This is mainly because sometimes, as in this case, the bush phone transmits on the same frequency as the movie channel the town is pirating.

I spend a couple of hours with Bridge in town. They are the most pleasant hours I've spent with my wife for a long time. We walk through the frozen streets hand in hand, the cold nibbling our faces. At every alley we cuddle like teenagers, partly due to the cold. It is fantastic, and as I hold the two of them in my arms I give thanks.

Bridge has been staying out on the gold creeks in a little cabin that is warm and comfy. She loves the walk to work everyday and says it's an opportunity for her to contemplate the little miracle within. Being pregnant has also given her a new outlook on her job of caring for the pregnant mums of Dawson. She is now in the 'at risk' club herself and loving every minute.

Bridge's job takes her right into the homes of the locals in Dawson. She is a family support worker for families who are pregnant or who have babies under a year of age, which means developing very quickly a trusting relationship, mostly with women. She finds this quite easy as the women she meets she holds in awe, and this must have transmitted unconsciously to them.

She also works in a local bar and would laugh because she would meet the women of the town by day and then their partners by night. She felt it was a real privilege to be welcomed right into people's lives and enjoyed that trust very much, especially when it came to looking after their tiny babies.

Without having to say it, Bridge obviously enjoys her time without me very much and even looks forward to it. She always seems to try and challenge herself more when I'm not around. It makes sense, I guess, being one person is very different from being a partnership. I think that we are very lucky to still be together. It hasn't been easy, we've had to work at being flexible and open, so that our partnership changes as we as individuals change. Whether it's a wild skidoo ride, spraining her wrist from wood hauling, or having some life-haunting, awakening in the middle of the night, it's always great to hear her tales and to watch her trying to make sure that I'm hearing what she's telling me. Our reunions are the best, fun and full of fresh tales.

We go shopping for relatively fresh lettuce and other veg to restock the cabin but before I know it the sun has dipped below the mountains and the streets are in shadow. It's time I crossed back to the cabin before it and everything in it freezes. The problem with a woodstove is that you can never leave it for long. I leave Bridge in town because it is still not totally safe to cross, especially as she's pregnant. I want it to be impossible to return, so I can stay the night with Bridge and the baby, but Boris is alone, and I want to get back to work so I can have some sort of warm comfortable home for my family when they come home, I hope, for Christmas.

I make it back without any trouble but the lettuce has

frozen. I'm feeling very alone and very cold because the stove has gone out. The amount of work I have to do before Bridge can come here is incredible. We only have a skeleton of a cabin, no kitchen, no bathroom, no bedroom and no furniture. And now we're going to need another room for Denzil (my name for the baby).

December 20th

I don't know how cold it is because the thermometer is outside on a spruce tree and I'm still in my sleeping bag and don't intend to get up for a long time. The thought of all the work I have to do is overwhelming so I'm hiding from the feeling of failure. I hate that feeling. No matter what you do it's always there ready to lunge at you and boast about how stupid you've been. Life is all about choices, but living with the choices you make is sometimes harder than making them. I've just been thinking about England and all the people there that we used to know, our friends and family. They would be thrilled to know we are going to have a baby. I miss them all terribly and it would be so nice to have them around at a time like this.

How simple life would be right now if I had continued on my merry way drawing cartoons and finding life comfortable. We would have our family around us, who would buy little designer outfits from M&S for our new baby. Our mothers would be knitting booties and hats that we wouldn't actually need. I would be decorating a nursery with fluffy Disney animals and a lacy cot with homey-smelling blankets. We would have bought a bottle of Miltons to clean all the surfaces of our 'kitchen', and have a year's supply of nappies with a neat odour-free disposing system. Instead of having to build a nursery in ridiculously low temperatures, I'd be decorating one. Choosing wallpaper instead of trees. If I were cold I would get off my comfy sofa during a commercial break in 'Friends' and turn the thermostat up a notch, or maybe even two.

I would not be lying here on my own, freezing, in the dark and talking to a short legged dog who passes the time by farting. The plastic on the windows has a quarter inch layer of frost on it. The temperature on the floor of the cabin is below freezing, judging by my boots frozen to the floor. And the lettuce has still not defrosted into slime. How on earth can we bring a child into this? Right now I would much prefer to be buying armloads of talcum powder for sensitive buttocks than contemplating the thought of building another room on my Frankenstein cabin.

I have four days before Bridge will really insist on coming home. That means in four days I have to put a proper track across the ice, make a bed, find a door for the cabin, cut enough firewood for a week and clean the place of lumber, sawdust and off cuts so Bridge can at least sit down somewhere.

When I finally drag myself out of the warmth of my sleeping bag and go outside I am met by a pink world. The sun is just coming up and the snow radiates a pink glow. It is so inspiring that I go looking for firewood, and soon I have at least five days worth stacked and split at the cabin door. I even begin to tidy up a bit. Life is always better after a rant.

If I am not around to continuously feed the stove with wood it gives up, and everything becomes cold in the cabin within hours. When I arrive home from the frosty world outside, wanting a bit of comfort, there isn't any, so I stand over the stove with the cold seeping through my clothes and attacking my kidneys until things begin to warm up a little.

December 21st

I rise early and walk to the lookout with Boris to check on the state of the ice jam. It's still there and has grown considerably in size. It looks like the river will be crossable for a while. After some moose meat, I decide to have a go at putting a skidoo track across the ice ready for Bridge. It will take a lot of chopping and shovelling but I think it's possible. Once a track is in, it will become smoother with each snowfall.

It's far too much work for any civilized cartoonist. The ice on the river is like rock and takes several attempts to chop a sizable chunk off with an axe. I find it especially difficult trying to swing an axe with thick gloves on. The axe keeps twisting in my grip making me miss my aim and nearly embedding the axe in my shin. Luckily Brent and Black Powder Billy come down with the same purpose so the three of us hack a track all the way to the other side. It takes some navigating and has more hairpin corners than a Nintendo racetrack.

While I'm on the ice I see the slew - a slow shallow stretch of the river between an island and the main shore - is frozen over, and I remember the island has an abandoned cabin on its far end. I'm going to skidoo down through the slew tomorrow to see if I can salvage its door for our own cabin. It's great when everything comes together.

December 22nd

Just another day in the north. Several miles down the river on the skidoo I notice the ice beginning to crack open. I look back and see open water bursting through large cracks and plates of ice the size of small tennis courts, sink into the river, cutting off my return trail. I continue, hoping the ice will freeze before my return.

I reach the derelict cabin on the edge of the island and find the door hanging from its log frame by one ancient hinge. It is a turn of the century, panelled fir door in remarkable condition but shows signs of weather and the odd bear. I tie it to the back of the skidoo and make for home.

It isn't long before I can see open water stretching from bank to bank in the slew and my heart sinks. The river is rushing over fallen plates of ice and eating into the ice on the far side of the open water, creating a sharp jagged outline two feet higher than the ice I was on. There is no way around. I have to go across and quickly because darkness is imminent.

I cut a stick, then wade in to the numbing water to see how deep it is. I'm lucky, the deepest part is about thigh height. The skidoo looks a long way off through the steaming water, the only colour and lifeline I have in a bleak, white world. I cross back to it and untie the door. My hands and feet are numb as I go back into the frigid water and try to make a ramp with the door so I can get onto the higher ice. I scrape a lot of snow onto the door to weigh it down so the current doesn't move it, and pray the skidoo will start as I climb on. Once you get wet in this country it doesn't take long for frostbite to begin. The skidoo starts with the first pull of the cord and my spirits lift. If I make it across, I'll be in the warm cabin laughing about this within the hour.

I can't feel my feet but I'm not cold in the slightest, which is a worry, because one of the first signs of hypothermia is that you feel warm. My clothes are heavy with ice. Taking a deep breath I rev the skidoo and take off over the water. I focus on my make shift ramp, squinting through the icy spray, and hit it more or less on target. The skidoo comes to a sudden stop and I go flying over the windscreen and onto the ice. The ramp wasn't strong enough and the skidoo has wedged its skis tightly under the solid ice. The cold surges into my body and saps my strength. I think about trying to walk home but if I leave the skidoo it will be there till spring and probably won't survive the break up of the river. I try to lift the front of the skidoo but the engine compartment is full of water and the skis are jammed. Reluctantly, I step gingerly back into the water as the engine splutters and dies. Cold cutting into my legs, I reach through the water for the back of the skidoo and yank it several times with my fading strength, slowly working the skis free from under the ice. I crouch beneath the back of the skidoo, in freezing water up to my chest and heave the whole thing onto the shelf and out of the water.

Exhausted, I climb out and see the undercarriage has snapped. The left ski is lying at an acute angle to the body and the twisted suspension is broken and limp. It is like a bad drama. One disaster after another. All I want to do is get home. My hands are stiff and burning with cold. I am shaking uncontrollably as I wire the suspension back where it is supposed to be with the roll of haywire I always carry on the skidoo. Making wild promises to God I will never be able to keep I pull the start cord and the skidoo miraculously splutters into life. I climb on and begin a slow and extremely cold journey down river.

At the cabin I can't get off the skidoo, I am frozen solid to it. I really think I might die sitting right here outside the cabin in the dark. I cannot believe it, I am truly stuck by the seat of my pants. My mind is racing and I am really confused. I cuss the bear for eating the plastic cover and exposing the foam that now grips me. If I pee I might be able to defrost enough to struggle free, but I can't bring myself to pee my pants. What if it doesn't work and someone comes by tomorrow to find me dead and frozen to the skidoo by my own urine?

Sod it. After considerable deliberation I swiftly pee in my pants. The warmth is incredible and it works. I wriggle free of the skidoo and stagger into the cabin, only to find the stove has gone out.

I was in such a rush this morning that I forgot my axe and my pack, which has spare clothes, dried moose meat and fire lighting equipment in a waterproof box. If I had them with me I wouldn't have had to go though the undignified process of peeing my pants and risking hypothermia. I have learnt a very valuable lesson today. Nothing in this country is a quick trip. Every action needs planning.

Only hours later do I begin to get warm. I lie in my sleeping bag for ages, but my toes still feel as if they are a pack of frozen sausages. I have frost nip on my face, hands and feet and my whole body is burning and sore. The worst thing is, I have to go back to get the door.

December 23rd

I am really sore this morning. My hands and face are still burning and I've damaged the nerves in my legs. I've just cut a small Christmas tree and put it in the corner of the cabin, and dragged the skidoo inside to try and thaw it out. There is water everywhere. The stove has at last defrosted the walls, so they constantly drip. The skidoo must have half the river in it, which is now lying in a big puddle on the floor. I shoot two holes in the floor with the rifle to try and drain the water away but I have to keep putting a stick down the holes because they ice up pretty quick.

December 24th

Bridge is home. I walked into town to meet her this morning. She loves the cabin, even if she has to climb over the skidoo to get out of the door. I want to just wrap her in a blanket next to the stove and supply her with endless cups of hot chocolate and gherkins, but she's outside slicing up firewood with the chain saw.

January 8th

We had a lovely Christmas. Bridge bought me a little radio so we can keep up with the news, and I brought in the firewood. I forgot about Christmas until it was too late to buy any presents, but Bridge is happy because we have a cabin. Or so she says.

She started work again today and has to walk in and out

of town, which is about a seven-mile hike round trip. I walk with her to the river, through the dark silent woods, and watch as she walks out onto the dark ice and disappears into the black. She is to signal with a flashlight if she is in trouble and when she reaches the far bank. I stare out onto the dark ice for any signs of a light, for what seems like hours. Then a faint flicker of light waves far off in the distance. She's made it.

Having Bridge back has given me a new lease of life after the disastrous run up to Christmas. I'm still covered in frost blisters but am healing slowly, although I must look like a leper with a bad dose of acne. I decide to build a bed, not a fancy Ikea bed but a relatively comfortable one that does the important job of getting us off the floor, so tonight we shouldn't be so cold. We've ordered a mattress, pillows and duvet with flowery patterns on them from a Sears catalogue, one of the main ways to get modern things up here which has been around since the gold rush.

A friend of mine once wrote to Sears asking for toilet paper. They replied about a month later asking him to look in his catalogue for the order number. He wrote back saying that if he had the catalogue, he wouldn't need the toilet paper.

January 27th

I've finally fixed the skidoo. It's taken forever to get the necessary parts sent up from Whitehorse, the capital city. The chap on the end of the phone kept telling me that parts were hard to find for a machine of that vintage. I could have slapped him - the skidoo is the newest thing we own. I've been hauling firewood with it all day, which certainly makes life easier. I don't know why I didn't think of using it before. I hope I'm not turning into a northern version of Forest Gump. No, he can run, I smoked too much in my misspent youth for that sort of caper. Smoking is one of the many things we have had to give up. When the weather turns cold things like breathing are hard enough without coughing and wheezing from smoking.

Bridge is still walking to and from work everyday. The trail is better now and she's actually enjoying it. I'm not sure what women are supposed to be doing when they're four months pregnant, but I do find it worrying that Bridge gets up in the dark, in a cold cabin, and walks three and a half miles to work across a partly frozen river to start her day. I never thought Bridge would be pregnant up here and I don't know how to deal with it correctly.

We now have flashlight signals for 'help' and 'I've made it'. I wait at the lookout until I see her signal that she's safely across and then head back to the cabin to continue my building and practice my ever-growing vocabulary of swear words. I find it so frustrating building anything when I have absolutely no skill. The light is beginning to come back. It starts getting light at 9 a.m. and goes dark at 4 p.m. which gives me a couple of extra hours of work. The cabin is looking more and more homely and is getting very comfortable, although our fancy new mattress has not arrived yet. It is still pretty cold when it's 25 below outside. If we put a glass of water on the floor, it is frozen solid in a matter of hours. I just don't know how to stop the cold coming in. We do need to make the cabin bigger. Little Denzil, who is now showing, is due in July and already kicking for space. But I can't bear the thought of getting the chainsaw out and cutting a hole in the wall to build through.

January 31st

I'm in the doghouse. This morning I made the mistake of asking Bridge if she was enjoying being pregnant. She turned into a tearful, demented, plate-throwing lunatic, shouting at me for a least twenty minutes, in rather colourful language, about the fact that she hates it. Do I really think she likes wearing my trousers with half the leg rolled up? Do I think she looks even remotely sexy in them? I said, yes, of course you do, and she threw another plate and accused me of lying, which of course I was, but at least I was trying. She hates retaining water, I said don't drink so much, and another plate hit the wall. She hates craving gherkins when all we have is moose. I kept quiet and didn't mention the fact she shot it. She hates not being able to have a glass of wine, which apparently I am enjoying far too often. Hates swollen feet and everyone patting her belly. I said, I don't pat your belly, which unleashed more fury, as apparently I'm supposed to. I have a headache. I'm going to keep my gob shut from now on, and buy her some maternity clothes and gherkins if we ever get to a town that sells any. And maybe if it's possible try and get in touch with my feminine side, wherever I left her.

February 2nd

The trusty old weatherman on the radio says it's going to warm up to 10 below for the whole week. That probably means it's going to hit record lows for a month but I'm going to take the risk and cut an eight foot hole in the wall for the extension anyway. I already have the foundation and floor in place for the sixteen-foot square extension, but I'm just not skilled enough to build the whole extension in the right place without cutting the hole. Sometimes I wish I'd listened more in maths class.

There's no going back now. One side of the cabin is open to the elements, it's freezing in here and snow is blowing in. I've put a sheet of plastic over the hole to keep the heat in but judging by the frost that is creeping across the floor I doubt it's working. Right now cutting a hole in the wall in the middle of winter on the weatherman's say-so seems an incredibly stupid thing to do.

February 3rd

We froze last night. We couldn't even get the tiniest bit warm because the temperature dropped to 25 below. We ate our moose dressed in woolly hats and parkas, then scrambled into the sleeping bags in a vain attempt to find sanctuary. In the morning it's my job to stoke the stove and make the tea so it is relatively comfortable for Bridge to emerge from the mound in the bed, but I found getting out of bed this morning the hardest thing. It took a lot of coaxing for Bridge to get out of her sleeping bag, into Dorian Gump's World Of Freezing Stuff-Ups.

February 12th

Brent has just been up to warn us about wolves. He has had two dogs taken from his yard, eaten right off the chains, and someone in town had her dog snatched right in front of her while she was walking by the river. We've heard them howling quite a bit this year but I didn't know it was quite this bad.

February 25th

With the light coming back I'm getting the extension built quicker than I thought. The weather has been good to us, the temperature hovering around -15°C. At least things don't break at 15 below. 25 below might as well be 40 below if you're trying to work outside with generators, electrical cords and skill saws, as everything breaks, and the generator ices up so badly that I have to regularly pee on it to defrost it.

March 2nd

This morning we awoke to 35 below and it's still dropping. These are what we call 'get the dog in' times, when ice crystals float on a biting wind and a rainbow arches out of the valley. It's a beautiful morning, our nostrils fill with ice, our skin burns and trips to the outhouse have to be very short. Bridge looked as if she weighed 30 stone when we walked onto the ice this morning. She's bundled up in everything she owns.

I'm going to put an extra stove in the cabin while she's at work. We have to warm this place up, the cold is dragging our morale down to an all time low. Canned goods are freezing in their tins, snow traipsed in on the floor is getting thicker rather than melting and the batteries in the radio are so cold they don't work.

Last summer we found an 1891 cast iron cook stove in an abandoned cabin. It's left over from the gold rush, but is in very good condition and a real piece of art. Its decorative doors are embossed with spiralling patterns that wrap around a nickel centre. The ash plate reads 'Maple Cook' in an arch above 'James Stewart and co 1891'. By the looks of it they used to ship these things up here flat packed because the whole thing is put together with inter-locking segments and a few screws.

Once in, the stove throws out a remarkable amount of heat and we can cook on it too - it's got an oven and a large flat cooking surface. The chimney I've carved isn't exactly straight but what a difference it's made. Bridge is delighted. I just hope it doesn't crack under the strain of being 40 below one minute and 2000 above the next.

As we sit at the stove in silence the fire crackles away, heating a big pot of moose stew, our thoughts wander to the gold rush. Whose was this stove? Did they strike pay dirt? What had the stove seen in over a hundred years, how many lives had it saved? After over a hundred years it could still do the job it was designed to do. The way it creaked and groaned was almost musical. It should probably be in a museum, not defrosting a couple of pommies. It's an honour to have this antique in our cabin, linking us to this cursed yet beautiful land.

March 5th

Bridge is late getting home. Just as I am getting worried about her she struggles into the cabin. She is completely frosted up and worn out, her feet wet and half-frozen. The river has cracked in this low temperature and an overflow five inches deep is on the trail. It is quite unnerving to be on the ice when it cracks. It booms out from beneath, then moments later you hear the eerie sound of rushing water.

It is quite upsetting to watch Bridge's very painful warm up process. She cries in pain for a long time, then crawls into bed. Maybe we should go south until the baby is born.

March 8th

It's been 46 below for days now but at least the wind has stopped. It is so hard to describe how wonderful it is outside. The air smells of woodsmoke from the chimney, it's crystal clear and the full rays of the sun beam out from a low lying sun. The river valley is full of steam from the open water and the sky is full of colours, from dark blue to blood red. Everything is so bright and truly amazing. It makes anything you have to do ridiculously difficult, of course, except splitting wood. You only have to half-heartedly swing the axe and the logs shatter into several pieces.

We have stopped life as we know it. In this temperature everything breaks and you get tired really quickly. We're cabin-bound, shovelling wood onto the stoves. In some ways it's quite pleasant, almost relaxing. With Bridge being home from work during the cold snap I am finally getting the opportunity to supply her with hot chocolate as she sits by the stove, feet up, making winter clothes. We spend most of the days watching the incredibly bright sun move between mountains, casting long and distorted shadows across the brilliant snow. At night we watch the colour spectrum. A bright moon shines like a beacon, and the constellations spiral above our heads. Northern lights come out of nowhere and pulse across the stars before shrinking back behind the mountains.

We spend these cabin-bound times talking and reading to each other, drying moose meat, writing letters home and listening to the radio, especially the weather forecasts, intently waiting for the promise of warmer weather. Time and dates have no meaning. It's a very empowering feeling. I ask Bridge if she wants to go south or move to town until the baby is born, and am shut up very quickly. "This is our life, we chose it and we're going to live it." I knew she would say that but I had to ask for my own reassurance. The cabin is a lot warmer with two stoves but it still doesn't keep out this 40 below weather. Our feet are always cold, and if we sit on a chair we have to put up with the cold creeping over us like a draft. I don't know what we will do when the baby's born. Don't they spend most of the time on the floor?

We talk a lot during these times. We talk about what lies ahead, often with mixed emotions. The promise of a new life in our world is very exciting but also very worrying. Things like nappies, sanitary conditions, warmth, water and food are at the forefront of our minds. Then there's schooling, computers and socialising in the future. It's all very worrying and unsettling. We may have to give up on our quest for an idyllic life. The idealism we started with way back in Polperro seems foolish now we have someone else to consider.

March 17th

The weather has warmed to 20 below and we've managed to get the extension on the cabin sealed to the weather at last.

We have no windows yet, only plastic, but it has become part of our living space. Adding on two new rooms makes the cabin feel a lot bigger, though I still have to make some stairs to reach the upper one.

My next project is to make a bath. Bridge is so desperate for a soak she suggested booking into a hotel just for a bath. As well as our trusty green bowl, we've been using a bucket with a shower attachment hanging from its side that we fill with hot water from the stove. With no sewer system or plumbing we have to hang it from a tree outside. It's a great shower but makes for a hell of a lot of steam. You lather, wince, rinse then sprint back to the cabin wrapped in a towel before your hair starts to freeze. Bridge has stopped using it. She can't dash anywhere these days. Making a bath can't be that hard, can it?

March 20th

My bath is looking strange. I'm making it out of wood so it's going to be unique no matter what I do. I just hope it holds water. After buying building materials our money situation is almost non existent. It's amazing how expensive a box of nails is up here. Everything has to be ordered and sent up from the south, so the freight almost doubles the price of things.

Bridge is due to finish work in June so I've really got to get the cabin ready for the baby and find a job. I haven't been to town for a while so I'm not sure what is going on in the way of work. There's not much around in the winter but spring might mean a few odd jobs. Dawson is the only place I've been to where you're not judged on what you do for a living. You hear people saying, "I've worked enough this year, I'm going to the bush for a couple of months." I'm sure you wouldn't hear that too often on the London underground.

March 26th

A black bear skulked through the property today. It stopped at the cabin and stood looking at it for quite a while. Obviously as surprised as we are, that it's standing. We stood motionless inside, watching to see what the bear would do next. When it started to wonder over to the door I beat a few pots and Bridge sang 'I'm a Londoner'. Her singing worked, and the bear took to the hills.

It seems early for the bears to be out of hibernation but I suppose it is nearly April. This time of year is always a little unnerving as the bears wake up. They are very hungry and the berries are not out yet so there is little food around.

March 29th

I went to town today and got a job, for which they are paying me in gold, if we find any. The work involves digging a shaft down to bedrock somewhere out in the bush. It will be interesting but means leaving Bridge, who will have to work and run the cabin. I start first thing in the morning.

March 30th

I've seen it all now. This morning I packed my rucksack, kissed Bridge goodbye on the river and went to the oldest hotel in town to meet George, my new boss. The hotel defies the laws of gravity, leaning on numerous axis with a bottom floor that looks like it's sunk into the ground. It was built in the gold rush and is a real dive.

I thought I'd make a good impression by arriving early. I had to sit and drink beer with the owner of the hotel, apparently part of the enterprise, while he explained the necessary secrecy needed for this little project. I was a bit confused until he showed me behind the sloping bar and into a back room where George sat, a swearing wiry Frenchman in his late forties. He gave me a very toothless grin and beckoned me over to the five-foot square hole in the floor. The shafting was going on right there in the hotel through the floor of the oldest hotel in town.

Dawson itself has never been mined and is in a very good position to have millions of dollars of gold beneath it. If someone digs a hole today for a house foundation they sluice the dirt and regularly find gold. George excitedly explained the complicated system of ropes and buckets with which they were hauling up the frozen ground. I peered down the hole and saw a light 30 feet down and another little Frenchman called Pierre. I also saw a raven on a string tied to Pierre's foot. Apparently this was the Yukon version of taking a canary down a coalmine. An added precaution George told me, but not necessary. With great delight he then showed me why, switching on an ancient vacuum cleaner whose hose hung down the hole, controls set to blow instead of suck.

I wished them luck and left. The ground they were digging

was frozen and had been for thousands of years. It was so cold down there that Pierre was in his Parka and hat while he swung a pickaxe in a five-foot hole. They would be there forever.

April 5th

A glorious day. Spring is in the air for the first time and the winter snow is shrinking fast. The sun is high in a clear sky and the temperature is -5°C. I've just come back from town where I found a job advert for a Park Ranger of a brand new Tombstone Mountain Park. The Yukon has no park system in place yet, so it really is a great opportunity. The job will help to protect 5000 square miles of true untouched wilderness. I'm not sure if I'm qualified but I brought some information home to study just in case.

April 6th

I'm getting really carried away with this bath I'm making. It looks like a cross between a large wine barrel and Santa's sleigh. Bridge is not sure what to make of it and keeps asking why we can't just book into a hotel. I'm going to have to put it on hold for a while as this continued warm weather is defrosting our meat supply and I need to do something about it.

We keep all our frozen supplies in a large wooden box outside, which works fine during cold weather but is a different story when it warms up. I banked snow around the box yesterday to try and insulate it but it doesn't seem to be enough. The sound of dripping water is a sign that winter is behind us. Although winter is cold and hard work our lifestyle is set up to cope, and we depend on it. It opens up the country by freezing the rivers, it keeps our meat frozen, it's easier to get around with dogs and skidoos, and water is not a problem because of the endless supply of snow.

April 17th

I think Bridge is finally enjoying being pregnant. She loves to walk to work. She says something great happens as she walks down through the woods and across the frozen river. She wears a lovely smile and happiness flows from her. I still wish that she would slow down a bit. Today she was felling trees and helping me drag them out of the bush for the icehouse we're making. The icehouse is the only way we are going to keep our meat frozen. We've dug a big 10-foot hole into a bank and are now building a log structure within it. We then hope to fill it with ice chunks from the river and hope it stays frozen all summer. Only time will tell. If it starts defrosting we can always dry the meat. We do quite a lot of this anyway because it makes great food for the trail and doesn't freeze. But it's not quite the same as a juicy steak the size of your dinner plate.

April 19th

Life is waking up quickly. The sun is now shining for 14 hours a day and beating back the snow, hinting at easier times ahead. It's a great feeling after the long cold winter.

The depleting snow has some drawbacks, mainly our water supply, which we have to go further and further to find. There's a creek about eight miles away that usually runs most of the winter, but it's at the bottom of a really steep hill. Once there we cut a hole in the ice with an axe and scoop out the water into five-gallon buckets. It takes a few hours to do a water run on the skidoo so I'm not sure I want to finish the bath yet.

Break up is looming once again. The ice on the river is getting increasingly risky to cross. At the moment we are crossing on foot, dragging the canoe, in case we go through. But I think it's time Bridge moved to town for her own safety.

April 22nd

I should work for Ikea instead of being a roughty toughty adventurer. With Bridge now in town I'm building kitchens, chairs, tables, you name it. I've just finished making a table out of scrap wood salvaged from a job site in town a year ago. It looks great, but above all, it works. Bridge can put her feet on it and paint her toenails red if she ever felt inclined to do such a strange thing.

April 27th

I have been crossing to and from town every other day to check the mail to see if I got the Park Ranger job. One of the great improvements in our lives is that the only mail we receive is letters from friends and family. Not one bill or mail shot lurks for us in the post office, waiting to upset our day.

It appears I have a written exam tomorrow morning to qualify for an interview. I can't believe it. For quite a while now I've been studying the history of the Yukon's Park objectives, the planning of the Tombstones and the Government acts and regulations, so hopefully I know a little. My main concern is the river. I put a foot through the ice on the way back to the cabin. It's getting very thin and almost impossible to cross. I'll see what it's like tomorrow.

April 28th

I manage to cross the river and sit my three hour exam. Afterwards I go to see Bridge and am horrified. She has little hair on her head, no eyebrows, first and second degree burns on her face and hands and very nasty third degree burns on her forearms. She had trouble starting the wood stove in the cabin she's staying in. After several attempts it kept going out so she found a can of camping stove fuel, which, of course, exploded as soon as she put it on. Poor Bridge, she looks terrible, and had to walk a mile to town before someone drove by and took her to the nursing station. She is still shaken up by the incident but apparently the baby is OK. I don't want to leave her but I need to get back to the cabin. This is the last time I am crossing until I can canoe.

After stopping off at the liquor store for a pack of nerve calming beer (that I can only just fit into my rucksack because of all the other less vital supplies like fresh veg) I venture out across the extremely rotten ice. I am almost across when it breaks beneath me, plunging me into freezing water up to my neck. It takes my breath away, I can't breathe or shout, and I fight hard to calm my panic. I then realise I'm not touching the bottom of the river, and I can feel the current pulling at my dangling legs. The base of my rucksack frame has miraculously caught on a thin ledge of ice and stops me going completely under. But I am too scared to move. The canoe is floating down stream and dragging me off the ledge because its bowline is wound around my wrist.

In situations like this one you think of funny things. I'm thinking that the loaf of bread in my pack will be ruined. I can't feel the cold but can definitely taste the river water after swallowing what seemed like gallons. Gathering my thoughts I gently pull on the bowline and the canoe glides towards me. I think it's going to pull me off the ledge but I manage to get two hands on the gunnel. My rucksack is so waterlogged that I can't pull myself into the canoe, so I unclip the hip belt and slip out of the shoulder straps. It falls with the current and disappears below the ice.

I am left hanging on the side of the canoe, which drifts 20 feet before stopping on the ice down stream. I haul myself in and begin to get very, very cold. With a hand on either gunnel, one foot in the canoe and the other propelling it along like a scooter I manage to reach the bank. I stumble back to the cabin.

It's been a gloriously sunny day but as soon as I reach the door of the cabin a snowstorm starts. Almost as if the Yukon is angry I got away.

May 2nd

The ice broke today. I awoke to its echo smashing into the cliffs in the river valley. Boris and I walked to the lookout to watch the spectacular action. I'm going to wait a couple of days until the river is free of floating bergs before I cross in the canoe to pick up Bridge.

May 5th

I canoed to town today to pick up Bridge. I also found out I have an interview next week for the Park Ranger position, so I'd better have a shave and rid myself of the bush look I seem to have developed.

May 10th

Bridge needs to get to town everyday to go to work so I've been walking with her to the river and then canoeing her across to town. We usually cross the strong current by canoeing up the shore in the eddies. Once we're level with the mouth of the Klondike and the south end of town, we turn into the main current and paddle like hell until we reach the other bank somewhere in the north end of town. Today was a nightmare. The wind was howling up the river from the north, blowing sleet sideways. When we turned into the current the river tried to push us north while the wind pushed us south. The two combining forces tipped the canoe at a 45-degree angle and we took on a lot of water. I thought we were going to sink, it was impossible to steer out of the way of the bergs and the sleet was hitting us so hard we couldn't open our eyes. Bridge, sitting in the bow, had to lean over and around her belly to paddle.

When we reached town I loaded the front of the canoe

with rocks to replace Bridge's weight and keep the bow low in the water for the return trip. Bridge protested strongly at the amount of rocks I put in, then waddled up the bank mumbling about her weight.

May 15th

The ferry went back in today, a sure sign of summer arriving. It's now time to find the truck, dig it out of hibernation and start learning to drive again. It's also time for me to think about starting work in two weeks as Park Ranger for the Tombstone Park. Yes I got the job! It must have been the tie I bought from the second hand shop. A tie is something only the bank manager wears up here. I actually thought I'd blown it at the interview, as trying to look intelligent is something I haven't done since meeting Bridgets' Father. When apparently I smiled like Mr. Blobby and laughed like Norman Wisdom.

June 2nd

Life has really taken a different turn. Bridge is at the cabin, I hope taking it easy. I am exploring the most amazingly beautiful mountains and arctic tundra and getting paid for it. The only drag is I'm away from home quite a bit, as I discover and map new routes through the jagged mountains.

And very jagged they are. The natives' name for the Tombstone Mountains is Dhhal Ch'el, which translated means, 'among the sharp, ragged, rocky mountains'. It's only since the gold rush that they were called the Tombstones after one mountain in the centre that looks like a tombstone. I am the Ranger Rick you see on telly chasing Yogi and Boo-boo out of campers' picnics.

Though here there are not a lot of campers. No one but a handful of hard core extreme outdoorsy types get into the range, though some more moderate types stay at a campground by the Dempster Highway, a gravel track winding through the arctic to Inuvik, an Eskimo town on the north coast of the North West Territories. Most of the time it's just caribou, wolves, grizzly bears and me.

For the first time in my life I actually enjoy having a boss. He says things like, "Dorian, I've booked a chopper to fly you into Deadmans Gulch so you can find a route out," or, "I hate to ask Dorian, but could you climb the mountains north of Grizzly Creek and find a pass down to the lake?" And to think that once upon a time the only dare devilish thing I did while making a living was to try a new type of ink.

June 11th

The summers are truly a magical time in the Yukon, hot and dry and timeless. It doesn't go dark so you can be sitting on the deck at midnight and swear it's only six o'clock in the evening. Bridge has a fair size vegetable garden, which is keeping her busy. It's full of potatoes, carrots and, for some reason, an awful lot of turnips. Our icehouse seems to be working well, everything is staying relatively frozen and when I'm home I build the cabin. Life is really quite perfect.

June 14th

Bridge and I are sitting on the deck talking and relaxing in the sun, when a rumble of thunder comes from the east. We watch as a huge black cloud, accompanied by a warm wind, steals the sky. Lightening snakes through it and seconds later another loud clash of thunder shakes the trees. We're nervous. Thunderstorms are a real hazard. Little rain falls with them at this time of year, so a well placed lightening strike can cause a forest fire that could leave us homeless or worse, smouldering.

The storm moves across the sky and out over the Klondike valley. After waiting for the smell of smoke and detecting nothing but Boris, we sigh a big sigh of relief. We've built our cabin on a valley ridge, with thick, dark, spruce forests surrounding us for miles. There's only a small road that leads to our property, so if a fire starts anywhere in the nearby hills it will naturally draw up to us.

Another hazard we've discovered is porcupines. Last night we were lying in bed when we heard some amazing howling coming from the deck. I jumped out of bed, grabbed the gun and flung open the door to Boris, whose snout was covered with porcupine quills. Below the deck was a chubby porcupine scoffing the bottom step like it was a stolen portion of fish and chips. I tried to shoo it away by shouting some inventive names. It didn't reply because its gob was full of my front step so I gave it some lead to chew on then went to help Boris, who had over 50 quills stuck deep into his nose, gums, tongue, snout and face. Blood was everywhere. I literally had to sit on him for over two hours while I pulled them out with my trusty leatherman. Some I couldn't get, they were far too deep.

June 17th

Sometimes I wonder whether Boris was born with any grey matter at all, or that his synapses are not stimulated by electrical pulses like every other warm-blooded creature but by the urge to smell bad. He has just crawled back to the cabin as if he'd slipped a disc. By the looks of him he's found the dead porcupine that I thought I hid rather well and taken the liberty of rolling in it. Another fun filled evening of plucking Boris awaits.

July 2nd

I've just pitched my tent on top of a mountain looking down on one of the many unnamed lakes in Foxy Creek. My radio crackles into life and fills my silent world with a metallic voice. It's my boss, Gord. He sounds like a man about to push the little red button that would end the world. "I've been trying to get hold of you since yesterday. Bridge has been taken very ill and is going to be air lifted to hospital in Whitehorse. The baby is in great danger and needs to be born immediately. Bridge is refusing to go until she sees you. Get to your wife quick!"

I am two days into the backcountry. It will take me forever to get to my truck and another two hours to drive to Dawson, not to mention a further seven hours to get to Whitehorse. I look around and complete and utter despair takes over me. I am on top of a wonderful mountain with a million-dollar view and it's the last place on earth I want to be. An overwhelming surge of helplessness flows through my body. I get up and start running down the mountain.

As I run, my mind races. Losing the baby was not an option. We would never forgive ourselves. I stumble over boulders and slippery shale as I negotiate steepsided tarns and creek gullies. I slip and fall constantly, struggling to look for the best footing. I slow to a fast walk as my knees begin to feel every jolt of foot. It is a wonderful day, beauty surrounds me and the wonders of nature are everywhere. I hate it, and want to cry with worry. Six hours later I drop out of the rocky, jagged mountains and onto the undulating tundra. I can see the truck way off to the east. A spot of brilliant red surrounded by brown tundra as far as the eye can see. I sit and rest for a while by a gurgling mountain stream, gulping handfuls of ice cold water in between gasps for mountain air. My body is hot and vibrating with adrenaline. My legs ache, my feet are sore and I feel completely sick with worry for Bridge and our unborn child. It's a sickness that almost cripples me, and I still have a long way to go.

Moments later I start running again. The going is a little easier on the tundra until I drop into a gully and have to follow a creek full of thick willows. I see a grizzly bear about a hundred yards away working its way up the stream towards me. I stop and wait to see if it is a sow and cubs. I can't see, get angry and shout. Seconds later the bear stands up and looks over the willows, its ears pricked, nose smelling the air. I wave my arms and shout again, and the bear disappears. I hold my breath for a few very intense seconds, bracing myself for an attack. I breathe a big sigh of relief when I see it charging out the other side of the willows and over the ridge. It is a young bear, alone and with no cubs. I run back into the willows and continue my descent.

Three hours later I am fumbling in my pocket for the keys, praying the truck will start. It does, and I speed along the lonely gravel road towards Dawson.

A forest fire is raging somewhere to the south and smoke hangs thick in the air like fog as I drive into town. An ambulance is waiting outside the nursing station when I throw open the double doors. I am escorted through the tiny centre to where Bridge is lying on a bed. She looks at me and smiles a worried smile as her eyes fill with tears. I hold her hand and kiss her forehead. A doctor comes scuttling into the room and shuts the door secretively. She explains that Bridge has a severe case of Toxemia and has to lie flat to try and keep her blood pressure down. If they cannot stabilise her blood pressure, they will have to get the baby out within hours or it will die.

The doctor leaves and an ambulance crew swarm into the room, hook Bridge up to all sorts of computers and wheel her into the ambulance to take her to an awaiting medical plane at the airport. I try to hitch a ride but am told there is no room on the plane. The emptied room goes quiet, and I sit on the bed trying to compute. I've just hiked up a hill for two days, run down it in nine hours and driven two hours to see my very ill wife for a fleeting 20 seconds before they whisk her off to hospital for a caesarean, which will mean our baby will be a month premature. An operation that I am going to miss because there's no room in the plane. And it takes seven hours to get to Whitehorse if you're Damon Hill on a straight road. I begin to lose it.

I am very hungry. I notice Bridge hasn't eaten her hospital meal. A nurse comes in to clean up and goes to take the chicken, and I turn into Miss Piggy with the table manners of a Viking. I snatch the plate from her hand and shovel the contents into my mouth while I stomp out of the station and into my truck. I'm going to the airport.

It is now raining very hard. The ambulance is in the middle of unloading a stretcher-bound Bridge onto a little jet plane when I arrive. The sky is blazing red with the glow of forest fires and water bombers are taking off every 60 seconds. As the crew struggle to get her through the tiny door of the plane, Bridge lifts up the blanket protecting her from the rain, looks directly into my eyes and mouths the words, "You owe me!"

Minutes later the little plane is disappearing behind the mountains and I am getting soaked. I jump into the truck and begin the seven hour journey to Whitehorse general hospital, wiping the rain from my eyes and praying Bridge will have the strength to hold on until I get there.

The road seems to go on forever as I drive out of the rain and smoke into the midnight sun. I think that I could very well be a father right now. I am almost out of petrol when I finally see the mountains that surround Whitehorse.

I reach the maternity ward where Bridge is lying flat in the bed. She bursts into tears when I enter the room. Her blood pressure has levelled off but is still very high, and she has struggled to keep the doctors from operating. She wants me with her and to have the baby naturally. The doctors have agreed to wait and induce her when I arrive. I am in the room a full minute before the nurses swarm in to begin the inducing process.

July 4th

We are now the proud parents of a healthy, baby boy called Jack Julian Amos. 'Denzil' didn't seem to suit him. Bridge held out to the last and delivered him naturally and with no drugs. The doctor put him on Bridges' stomach and within half an hour he crawled, by his own means, up to her breast, where he seems to have become a fixture.

I can honestly say he is the most perfectly beautiful thing I have ever seen. When I hold him in my arms and watch his little heart beat as he sleeps I finally know why we are putting ourselves through this adventure. It's all for him. It's so we can face life head on and live it deliberately. It's so we're not scared of life, it's so we can be strong, able to weather any storm and take on any challenge. It's so we as a couple have an unbreakable bond, enabling us to be resourceful and loving parents. It's so we know what life is and can pass on our knowledge and bring him up in a world full of freedom, natural wonders and adventure. It is for the future.

Part III

We were anxious about leaving the security of the hospital and Whitehorse with all its modern facilities. But when we reached our land with little Jack wrapped in a blanket, the trees waved in a warm breeze, welcoming us back. Boris greeted us with enthusiasm outside the cabin, which stood tall and proud, 'sanctuary' written all over it. When we walked in the door with Jack our life was complete, in a way that we hadn't known was possible. All of a sudden the cabin, our land and the Yukon was not just a dream or a struggle, it was our life. The cabin did its job wonderfully. We felt relief as soon as we opened the door and relaxed once inside. It felt like home.

From Bridget

Does any new mother have an inkling about the huge change a new baby brings into her life as soon as it is born? The limits to your freedom begin in pregnancy, with no drinking, no smoking, no partying and eating the right foods rather than what you really want. But that is only the tip of the iceberg. Our search for adventure had brought me face to face with life, but little did I know how little I was still actually living until Jack was placed on my stomach and crawled to my breast. It changed everything.

Day in, day out, my life is no longer my own, but it doesn't matter now. I am important primarily as Jack's carer, and everything else comes after that. I feel that my life will never revert to the egocentric state it was in before. Life is important because of Jack; my inner stability, strength and calm are all important because of Jack.

It didn't happen over night, it took a lot of adjusting.

The loss of my freedom to go wherever, whenever as an independent person washed over me in waves of icy water, becoming increasingly colder and shocking. I had no time to myself, none, none, none, none. I considered myself a single mother, and what a hard job that is. Dorian was in the mountains for days, sometimes weeks at a time and would get home exhausted and just want to sleep. That we had no modern conveniences or family around lost its significance as the daily adjustment to motherhood took centre stage.

The cabin did feel homely. Looking back at pictures though, I don't think anyone else would perceive it as such. All our walls were still pink insulation under clear plastic, the floor was plywood, the ceiling grey plastic. There were no doors, just sheets for privacy, and no real kitchen or bathroom. There was also an eight foot by 12 foot hole in one wall, the roof leaked and the outhouse was 20 yards through the trees, but none of it mattered. It was probably a good thing we were here in the bush outside Dawson, because anywhere else people would think we were mad to bring a baby into such a place. But here people tend to accept that surface things are not as important as what goes on inside, such as a person's ability to look after a newborn baby and really, was Jack aware of anything except the need to be held, fed and not left alone?

We had no formula or cows milk for Jack. We took a risk that his mum would provide everything he needed. There were a few anxious moments during the first couple of days, as Bridget's milk took a while to come through and we worried that Jack was getting hungry because he was so little. He had arrived three weeks early and weighed only five and a half pounds. Our little miracle looked tiny, vulnerable and weak. But, the calorie rich colustrum (pre-milk) kept him going until the breast milk arrived and he grew into a more normal-looking baby in no time. Nature knew what she was doing and right away he was putting on a pound a week.

Jack was with us constantly for the first few months. He was virtually never put down. When we held him we took our shirts off so there was a constant skin to skin contact, a natural reassurance to him that he was safe. Bridge shone with womanly brilliance, so patient, gentle and full of love. Jack was not an added chore to the already extensive list of things she had to do in a day. He was an extension of her. She carried him everywhere while she tended the garden, fed the dogs, cleaned the cabin and cooked the meals.

From Bridget

Women know that we'll do what needs to be done, as a matter of course. There are no heroics in this, I believe it is in our nature, part of our power. A friend of mine up here told me how one day her husband came home from work to find her breastfeeding their baby whilst taking a lasagne out of the oven. When he acted surprised she said, "this is the way things get done."

I had to carry Jack with me so I could still be doing things rather than just sitting with him all the time. I remember the feeling of accomplishment after I'd successfully completed the washing up for the first time whilst holding Jack. The ingenuity it took just to wash a few dishes was quite astonishing. I'm not great at sitting and just being. Each time I managed to do some of the chores with Jack it felt great, which could just as easily be the reason for my 'womanly brilliance'!

Breastfeeding played a big role in my ability to carry on

with a relatively normal life. I would walk for miles with Jack and not have to stop to feed him - it was fantastically simple, and I loved it. I would change his position slightly to the side, maybe have to support his bum with an arm, then undo a couple of buttons and voila! He could feed, and I could carry on meandering through the woods, albeit loudly to try and scare the bears.

One day I came home after being in the mountains for five days. I was a little apprehensive to see if Bridge had coped all right. I opened the door of the cabin and there she was, sitting in a rocking chair next to the stove, singing a lullaby while she watched Jack feed. Only when she looked up at me with tears in her eyes did I really understand how happy she was. It filled me with immense pride and contentment.

The fact that we had no running water, electricity or phone was totally irrelevant. We also had no bottles to warm, no formula to heat, no dummies to sterilise, no baby monitors to watch, and initially no baby clothes to wash because there was a heat wave so we didn't need to dress him. It was brilliant, though a little scary. Parenting according to instinct and common sense made us do what we felt was right, it made things simpler and made our baby our life. But this didn't always sit easily with the Victorian parenting values we'd been handed down, and there was always a nagging doubt in the back of our minds as to whether we were doing things right.

From Bridget

I really love not having a phone, it goes along with keeping life simple but it does have its drawbacks. If I'm concerned about Jack I can't just pick up a phone and make an appointment with the doctor. I have to walk to town with him and see if they can squeeze me in sometime that day.

Medical services are pretty good in Dawson. Although the doctors are not always on duty, there is a nursing station that is open most of the time. The nurses are very helpful and I feel better about raising Jack here knowing they are there. Because the Doctors don't work out of regular hours though, the nurses have to deal with all out of hours emergencies, and if the situation is serious enough the patient is flown to Whitehorse, like me towards the end of my pregnancy. All pregnant women in the Yukon outside Whitehorse are considered 'at risk' and so have to go to Whitehorse to give birth. At the time I was already feeling very undignified because I was as wide as I was tall and unable to elegantly sit, lie down or get up. Having the ambulance men manually move all 160 lbs of me from bed to stretcher to plane added insult to injury and I felt naked, embarrassed and completely out of control. It was good preparation for childbirth.

We have a few visitors when they are able to cross the river, which is both an advantage and a disadvantage. I think we get so many because they don't have to call and formerly ask to visit. The best visitors are a family, so Jack gets interaction with other children, which he loves. I worry about him being isolated and am always pleased when there is an opportunity for him to play with other children.

One September day I returned to Dawson after two weeks

in the Fishing Branch River. I'd had the most amazing experience crawling into Grizzly bear caves, which had been carved into limestone rock over billions of years. The bears hibernate in the caves and the rock inside is covered with hundreds of years of ice from their breath. It was a humbling experience and I felt amazingly lucky to be carrying out such research, but it diminished to nothing when Bridge picked me up at the chopper pad and I saw Jack smile for the first time. He smiled in response to Bridget's laughter and I saw a bond between mother and son that swelled my heart. Jack was responding, he was laughing and smiling, it was incredible.

I spent a lot of time taking Jack for walks in the surrounding woods while Bridge got some time to herself. I would sing to him for hours while his new eyes watched the natural world in wonder. He seemed not to take much notice of my singing but as soon as I stopped he would start to cry. I was astonished - usually the response to my singing is the other way around.

All too soon Freeze Up was looming. This time I was the one to stay in town and work while Bridge and Jack stayed in the cabin. My job is for ten months a year and I have November and December off. That meant that Bridge and Jack would be alone in the cabin for roughly two weeks until I could fly over by helicopter.

This worried me and I suggested they stay in town while I finished work. But Bridge pointed out that she would not do anything remotely as stupid as stuff her face with nails at forty below.

With a heavy heart I waved goodbye to my family from the last ferry to town. Jack was only three and a half months old, and Bridge had never spent Freeze Up over there, let alone with a baby. I had no way of contacting them. Did they have enough firewood? What if Bridge cut her leg with the chainsaw and couldn't get back to the cabin where Jack was lying? What if Bridge became ill and could not look after Jack? Brent had gone south for a dog race so there was no way she could get help.

The ferry docked and I walked off looking back across the river. I could see Bridge with Jack in a backpack walking back into the woods. It was snowing and the night was coming but it was already black in my heart.

I threw myself into my work, trying not to think about my family across the river. On my last day of work I booked a helicopter but the cloud was too low to fly, and by a cruel twist of fate it remained so for two weeks. Everyday I went to see Jon, the helicopter pilot, and every day he would laugh and say, "No way mate! Maybe tomorrow." Tact wasn't his greatest asset. I hung around town like the lost soul of a Klondike stampeeder, pacing the riverbank for hours watching for any signs of Bridge as the murderous ice bumped and growled its way down river.

Finally the weather lifted slightly. I ran to the chopper pad, where Jon was wiping his hands with an oily rag and smoking a cigarette. After the usual piss taking that Jon calls a greeting, he sauntered over to the door and looked up at the sky with mischievous eyes. He knew how anxious I was to get across the river but he was having fun. I'd flown with Jon quite a lot in the course of my job. He once got lost flying me through the mountains and we had scary moments flying sideways through the jagged tops with the rotary blades inches from the rocks. I still don't know if he did that on purpose.

Finally he offered to give it a go, and we took off and

swung over the Klondike up into the clouds. They were thicker than they looked from the ground and for a brief moment we were totally blind, but Jon continued talking to me in his endless mocking tone. Moments later the clouds parted like the curtains on a stage and we entered a stunning northern drama. Sunshine burst across the wiry landscape and spruce trees sagging with their winter snow blanketed the hills. Snaking through this was the Yukon River, its deep valleys shrouded with fog.

The cabin was still standing! Smoke was even coming out of the chimney, and fresh footprints led to the outhouse. We circled low and moments later Bridge came running out waving with little Jack in her arms, while Boris barked and twirled. Jon laughed. "You don't have to worry about that one, she's a winner mate. Has she got a sister?" "Just put me down," I said, as so much relief surged through my body that I nearly wept.

Inside the cabin I felt love bursting out from everywhere. Bridge danced with excitement and Jack put up with me swirling him around as the noise of the helicopter disappeared behind the mountains. We were all together once again in our home. It felt incredible.

From Bridget

I found the time by myself hard, especially in the first week. I didn't see anyone and I felt completely alone, yet I didn't have the freedom that comes with being alone, which made it more painful.

I now know, however, that it was the beginning of the end of my feelings of co-dependency.

When I was 18 and a fledging in the world I found and chose Dorian, the perfect partner for me. Aside from everything else that attracted me about him, he was mentally and physically strong, and so able to lead and look after both himself and me. It had worked exceptionally well for 13 years, but the time had now come to live up to my dreams of strength and independence.

Being alone during this time, totally responsible for Jack and myself, I came face to face with why I had never attempted to be alone before. It was exceptionally hard. Before coming to the Yukon I hadn't lived enough to develop the skills of courage and self-belief that I needed to bear my own company. I believe that life offers us many opportunities to learn such things, and it is our choice when and if we learn them. This time I didn't choose to back down or run away and hide in the thousands of ways I had taught myself. This time I endured.

By the time Dorian flew over the cabin a month later, I had learnt a lot about endurance. I learnt that it can be pushed deep and far and then deeper and farther still. I learnt that once I'd endured, I didn't have a ticket to all situations that required endurance, but what I did have was the confidence and belief in myself that I could endure. Something which will now be with me always.

As the skies cleared the temperature dropped and within two weeks we were trapped in our cabin. With temperatures of 36 below it was far too cold for Jack to spend more than a few minutes outside.

The cold marched into the cabin as well, and we could do nothing but stoke the stoves. We couldn't put Jack down on the floor, so he spent most of the time all winter on the table. We couldn't go for walks or mush dogs because it was far too dangerous to do that with Jack. Instead we succumbed to cabin fever, and for the first time the long cold winter got on top of us.

We lived in a dusky world for two months, lit only by the weak glow of our kerosene lamps. Jack cried a lot of the time. He didn't want to be put down at all, so we walked around and around and around the cabin trying to comfort him. He was taking all our attention and driving a wedge between us that we didn't notice until it was too late. We didn't so much argue with each other but bickered. We needed to get out and walk through the endless quiet forests for our own sanity. Jack took all our emotion, our strength and our love. It was very stressful.

From Bridget

I find it hard to admit that we had a hard time in our 'perfect world', but this was awful. Dorian and I failed to communicate and laugh, and there was lots of misunderstanding, self-centredness and bad behaviour. It was a miserable, cold world with no laughter, and very worrisome to be in it with a small baby.

We wandered around and around the cabin, avoiding each other's eyes and growing increasingly apart. It was miserable being cooped up, and we were both overwhelmed by the feeling that we were missing something. Life is like a loaf of bread, if it isn't used it becomes stale and hard. Which is what was happening to ours. Talking stopped, loving stopped, life stopped, until one day in late January.

It is 40 below and we have no meat, so Brent and I venture into the Tombstone Mountains to hunt caribou.

Although it is bitterly cold, it's an amazing day. The sun is bright and clear and it feels terrific to be in the white wonder of the mountains after the depressing cabin. We skidoo for miles across open tundra and over jagged mountains until we see and shoot four caribou in the late afternoon.

While I gut and clean the carcasses, Brent drives back to the highway to put a trail in, which will make it easier to drag the meat back. It takes me about an hour to dress the animals and prepare them for transport, then I wait.

Dusk moves in and a crescent moon peeps between the mountains in a purple sky. I rock backward and forwards to keep my body moving while the night bites at my face and my hands begin to curl and shut down with cold. I wait and wait and wait for Brent's return, fighting off an overwhelming sense of anxiety.

I put my feet inside the rib cage of one animal and sit on the others as night steals the mountains and the 40 below air creeps into my clothes. I have no way of telling how long Brent has been gone, but it must be hours. I hold my breath in the dark of the freezing night, listening for the sound of a skidoo. But there is nothing but total silence. For once it isn't welcome, only exciting the panic that is ready to erupt from my body at any moment.

The carcasses freeze solid, and my feet become very cold. What the hell has happened to him? I rub my cheeks with my bare hands. I don't have enough equipment to survive the mountain night at 40 below, and am unsure what to do next. Should I try and walk back to the truck, follow Brent's skidoo track or stay put in case he comes back from another direction? Whatever I do it's going to compound the problem.

Whatever that was. I decide to try and follow Brent's track, thinking that if I don't start to warm up soon I'll be like the caribou I'm sitting on.

I walk half an hour, trying to retrace my steps in the dark, when Brent appears over a rise, his skidoo light shining like the gift of life. I am flooded with warm relief, but pretty angry. What has he been doing? My body is shutting down. Did he stop for a sleep in the truck? I can't understand what has taken him so long.

He pulls up next to me and I am about to shout at him when I see he is exhausted. He shuts off the machine, throws his hat onto the snow and says, "I can't find the road!"

Anxiety shoots through my body. I work in these mountains daily but now as I turn around everything looks the same. Brent has been driving for hours over rough terrain and looks as if he's just run the London Marathon. I wait for him to come up with a plan but he sits there staring into the dark. "I don't know what to do," he mumbles, fiddling with the throttle of the skidoo. He's been living in this cursed land for a long time, I trust him, he always knows what to do. My guts twist with his words.

It is now pitch black and well below 40 below. My face is freezing and the cold has so stiffened my limbs that I'm not sure I'd notice if one just snapped off. "We have to find that road," I say, trying to think. "What the fuck do you think I've been trying to do for the last two hours? No Brent. We have to find that road. Lets leave the meat and work our way out of here."

Brent looks in the petrol tank as he wipes the frost from his face. "We'll be walking pretty soon," he says. I can tell he's scared. I have never seen him like this and it amplifies my fear.

I think I know the direction to go in but cannot be certain.

As I jump on the skidoo I try to sound positive and give Brent directions. We bump through the snow for another hour as the wind burns our faces and locks our joints. We come to a crest of a hill and look around. Nothing seems familiar.

We are totally lost. The skidoo steering is frozen and can only turn left. We are cold and hungry and fear is beginning to take a grip. In frustration Brent takes his axe and starts to beat the right ski of the skidoo. I try to stop him until I realise he is knocking the ice from the steering. The cold hangs heavy in the air and makes us crouch and huddle as if it is raining.

"We're going to have to try and survive the night," Brent says as he looks in the petrol tank for the last time. I find a snow bank and began to dig out a hole with a snow shoe, while Brent searches the desolate tundra for scraps of firewood.

Taking a brief break on the skidoo, I see truck headlights way off in the distance. It is fleeting, in-between two hills, but I am elated. The chance of seeing truck headlights on the Dempster highway in January in the middle of the night is something like a thousand to one. I shout to Brent and we decide to try for the highway.

We almost make it when we run out of petrol, but I'm back in familiar territory now and know the way. We walk the final three miles to the truck, parked on the side of the road like an oasis in the desert.

Town is shut up when we reach it. We drive along Front Street and down onto the river ice. Shining across the ice, our headlights pick out Bridge with Jack in her arms, walking to town to enlist a search party. She bursts into tears when she realises it is us.

After our little adventure we came to our senses. We knew that being stuck in the cabin was, in a different way, just as dangerous as the weather outside and took every step to avoid it. We bought a bigger skidoo so all three of us could fit on it comfortably. We took it in turns to mush the dogs. We worked out ways of dressing Jack for the winter air, and Bridge carried him on her back in a sling with a big Parka over the top. He would doze for hours on long skidoo rides into the bush.

To say life with Jack in this northern world is difficult would be missing the point entirely. Picking up a wet fish is difficult, getting Boris to heel is difficult, but after our journey we have few difficulties. Life itself is never difficult, it's exciting and adventurous, because of the way we look at it.

Our lack of facilities only means that we are raising Jack as naturally as possible. Instead of a soother or teething ring he chews dried moose meat. Instead of a bottle of milk he has his mother. We have no carpet in the cabin so it's not a total disaster if he has a mishap on the floor. And with no telly to plonk him in front of we spend many hours reading to him, walking and playing with him. It is truly living.

From Bridget

The caribou trip knocked sense into both of us. It was very difficult to keep my mouth shut about how stupid they had both been to get into that situation. That four caribou had been shot for no reason was also awful. They were very fortunate to have escaped unscathed.

Remembering carrying Jack on my back under the Parka always makes me smile. It was simple, effective and freeing. It also shocked people, which was kind of fun sometimes.

When I got to town people would see the hunchback from the other side of the river get off her skidoo and ask where Jack was. I would turn around, and they would gasp. "Can he breathe?", they'd say, and I would smile and nod my head. What more could a baby want than to fall asleep warm against its mother?

I did hear on the radio recently a very tragic story of a couple who lived in the bush. They were going from one cabin to another by dog sled, and bundled up their six-month-old baby into 'the basket' of the sled. When they arrived at the cabin the baby had suffocated. I pray, as every mother does, for something like that not to happen to us.

Living a deliberate, free and challenging life has bought about some powerful realisations. Only with time have we really begun to understand them, because somewhere in our past, probably in the pursuit of money or by endlessly following rules and regulations, we lost the thrill of really living.

Occasionally I look back and remember the life I had in England. As I'm dog sledding through the wilderness, or breaking trail with the skidoo over the mountains, or sitting on the outhouse surrounded by dark spruce touched by the morning sun, or picking my way across the rotting ice of the river. I had a good and honest life in England and I have to stop myself regretting those years. In an ideal life I would have been born here, amongst the endless spruce, but I wasn't, and that's ok.

Now moments of sheer joy are brought on by simple things, like a warm fire after a long trail home, or managing to get back to the cabin after falling through the ice on the river, exhausted, frozen but truly alive. It's moments like those, when life is running rampant through my veins and bursting out of every pore in my body, that I feel the most incredible, unstoppable strength and power. That's when I look back with regret, and it's only the regret of not looking for life sooner.

It's the power of being alive that is so evident in our world since we left England. It is the most incredible feeling when my body and mind unite. I genuinely feel invincible, and it leaves me bouncing around the cabin for a couple of hours. I don't want to be feeling like that all the time, of course, because it's often the result of a life-threatening encounter. But the fact that it's possible to feel like that here day to day is a gift we welcome and treasure cautiously.

I needed the time in England to appreciate what we have now. I know, now, how to think clearly and the value of believing in myself. In my past life I didn't really need to believe in myself because there was always a way out or someone there to correct my mistakes. There was always another job or the dole for some breathing space, no choice we made was ever life threatening. To live here and in this way we have to believe we can do anything, because the Yukon's waiting for our failure. The fantastic thing is, we discovered very quickly, we can do anything!

I also remember the people I knew before we left England, and the negative responses we received after we'd made our decision to leave. The people that surrounded us were our friends, but I can't help thinking how insular some of them were. They couldn't believe we were just upping sticks and moving on when our life was safe and comfortable, just like theirs. Safe and comfortable are all well and good but I now know contentment was missing.

I am still astonished by the statement 'you're getting too old to do that sort of thing'. It would probably have been easier to change our life when we were teenagers and not in our early thirties, but I would still be disco dancing in flares if I listened to that philosophy. We are now accomplishing things everyday we never thought possible, and with that comes the fantastic feeling of really being alive. Because we did not listen to the negativity that infests the safe, commercial world, we know what we're truly capable of and that is something we must know to sincerely live our life.

We have been in Dawson for four years now and still can't wait to get up in the morning and see what the Yukon will do to us today. We look at the surrounding hills and distant mountains and they always say something different to us. They look placid, inviting and beg to be explored, or they're dark, moody and shout to be left alone. Only the Yukon knows how she truly feels, and only a fool explores her without the respect that suits her stature.

The biggest change we have felt since entering the north is within ourselves. We know absolutely nothing is easy up here, and we've developed an inner strength to deal with that. At times we are complacent and lazy, although we can't afford to be. We're constantly getting at each other for being stupid and doing stupid things. The Yukon quickly crushes the weak and lazy, and we are often left humiliated by the bruising we get from her.

This is how she keeps herself pure and unspoilt. She has no time for people trying to manage her, change her or tame her. If you try to put concrete or tarmac onto her skin she will force the frost up and break it within a year. She is the only one who chooses who can stay and on what terms. If you don't comply it will cost you your life, or at the very least your mind.

The inner strength we've built up and continuously nurture

allows us to live with her. She opens up and shows us the way, only because we make time to listen. But I would be lying if I said every day was positive. There are times when the challenges and problems mount up and seem impossible to overcome. This happens regularly, and failure (mostly only temporary) is something we have grown to live with. But the Yukon always brings us time to re-build our strength and try again. Giving up is not a healthy option in this climate.

Everybody in the Yukon wilderness has this inner strength. It is a remarkable gift she gives us. It empowers us to overcome seemingly insurmountable problems in a calm, matter of fact way. I know of people who've been caught and injured in avalanches as they've crossed the mountains, and carried on as if the avalanche was a train delay or a traffic jam. The Yukon is the only place I know that this happens, because she takes the meaning of time out of our hands. Deadlines, meetings and appointments are all undertaken with the Yukon and her moods in mind.

The Yukon also enables people to be together with a loved one in a way few people are able to. When the weather is terrifying for days on end and people are forced to retreat to the sanctuary of their cabin, they sit and talk for hours without television or other outside distractions, the only light coming from the fire or the odd candle.

The best thing is being able to appreciate the little things. A rise in temperature, the echo of a whisper in an endless forest, the coming of dawn, the warmth of a fire, the touch of the sun or the call of the raven. They happen again and again but each time they are as priceless as the time before.

The Yukon is forever giving confidence, pleasure and knowledge, but with the giving she also takes. She has taken our entrenched thought processes and cast them into the wind. Striving for material wealth is pointless up here and has no value. We no longer judge people by what they do for a living, what car they drive or where they live. Instead we listen to what they have to say. We're interested in the way they treat others, whether they can surmount trouble and embrace challenges, and what skills we can exchange.

The Yukon wilderness stripped us naked on our arrival. She then gave us a chance. She feeds us with her wildlife, warms and shelters us with her forests, quenches our thirst with her waters, humbles us with her power. If we're prepared to work she will even put gold into our pocket from her rivers, but you must be willing to believe in her. The Lore of the Yukon can never be learnt. It must be understood.

Although we paid money for our land, we feel as if we don't actually own a single twig or grain of sand. The money we paid only states to a man-made government that we cannot be moved on. To walk among the ancient spruce that stand tall on the land and show the scars of hundreds of brutal winters and scorching summers, it is obvious we are only a fleeting chapter in the endless life of a sleeping beauty.

Our life is governed by the moods of the weather and the changing seasons. Spring is a time of rebirth, a very bright time. The sun is high in the sky, some days almost blinding, and the skies are clear and a brilliant blue. There's no more struggling through snow or huddling against the chilling winds. We dress differently, eat differently and think differently. A strange uplifting, carefree feeling floods back, and we watch with interest as the snow melts to see what it will reveal and free up. It is also a time of caution. The sun quickly weakens the ice on rivers and lakes creating hidden hazards. Bears are awake and hungry and the threat of forest fires is constant.

Summer is a time to relax, explore and work. It's a time of high energy, fuelled by the ever-present daylight. We don't seem to get tired in the summer and are often on the go for eighteen hours a day. The air is warm and full of the scent of spruce pollen. Woodland birds colonise the forests, singing and chattering from the shadows. The First Nations, the Indians, gather on one of their traditional sites on the river. In the tranquil summer evenings their rhythmic chanting and drumming rise from the valley and drift over the hills. Their strange song takes us back in time.

There is no rush in the summer because it doesn't go dark, so there's no need to have a schedule. Everything and everyone goes at their own pace. We spend a lot of time outside in our garden and we cook outside on an open fire. The freedom from time is fantastic.

Autumn is a time to prepare for winter, when we wind down and anticipate. The air cools off and the forests become a patchwork of gold as the birch trees change into their autumn colours. The coming of winter is a real pressure and we have to be prepared for it. It takes a long time to collect, cut and stack a winter's supply of firewood; to hunt, kill, butcher and store a winter's supply of meat. When tools are stowed, equipment stacked for easy access and materials protected from the snow, it's time to sit and wait for the first snow fall and welcome its brilliance and promises.

Winter is the best season of all, and one of extremes. It's a time for adventure, for hardship, for comfort. It's a time to take to the forests and rivers and explore their wonder. To catch up with neighbours and friends, enjoying good cooking and wholesome conversations deep into the night. It means brilliant moonlit nights, star-studded skies and the dance of the northern lights, but also cosy times in our cabin. The cold northern winters are only a real concern if you are not ready for them, and if you have to try and carry on living a normal life.

It's such a welcome change to be affected by the seasons. In England I hardly knew it was summer - I could tell only by the fact it was light when I started work and still light when I finished. What a waste.

The Yukon River has become a major part of our life. We have a healthy respect for it and take few chances. With so few roads it's essential for travelling, and works as a highway in the summer and winter, opening up the wilderness and taking us to hidden places. The thawing and freezing of the river are the most dangerous times, but they're special for all the people who live in the bush on the other side of town. We come together during these prolonged periods, when a trip to Dawson is impossible, and catch up over a bowl of moose stew. There's something very calming about sitting in a neighbours' cabin during freeze up, surrounded by the smoke from the fire, the smell of drying clothes and burning candles. Stories about surviving helicopter crashes, boats sinking, avalanches or being lost in the bush are bantered between bearded folk who are not surprised by anything anymore.

We have met some wonderful, incredible people on our travels and many have become friends, but the best friend of all is a little dog I met at the pound, Mr. Boris Lovelock. He shares the same lust for life as we do. When he first came to us he had little hair around his neck where his chain had rubbed for most of his life. He longed for freedom just as we did, and now he has the run of the Yukon. I often watch him sitting on the porch looking into the woods. He knows they're there to explore any time he wants but sometimes he just wants to sit and admire them, just like us.

To some we've done nothing adventurous at all. We haven't climbed any mountains, discovered a long lost Tasmanian tiger or ventured into unmapped jungles. All we did was get out of our armchairs and greet the world with the enthusiasm it deserves. And it's that that's changed our lives.

I didn't intend to write any of this down, I just kept a diary for our own memories. But if our story motivates just one person to go and try something different, to find a moment of pure happiness, it will have been worth it. Adventure is everywhere and can be anything. It's really just the way you look at things.

FOOD

BRIDGET'S STORY

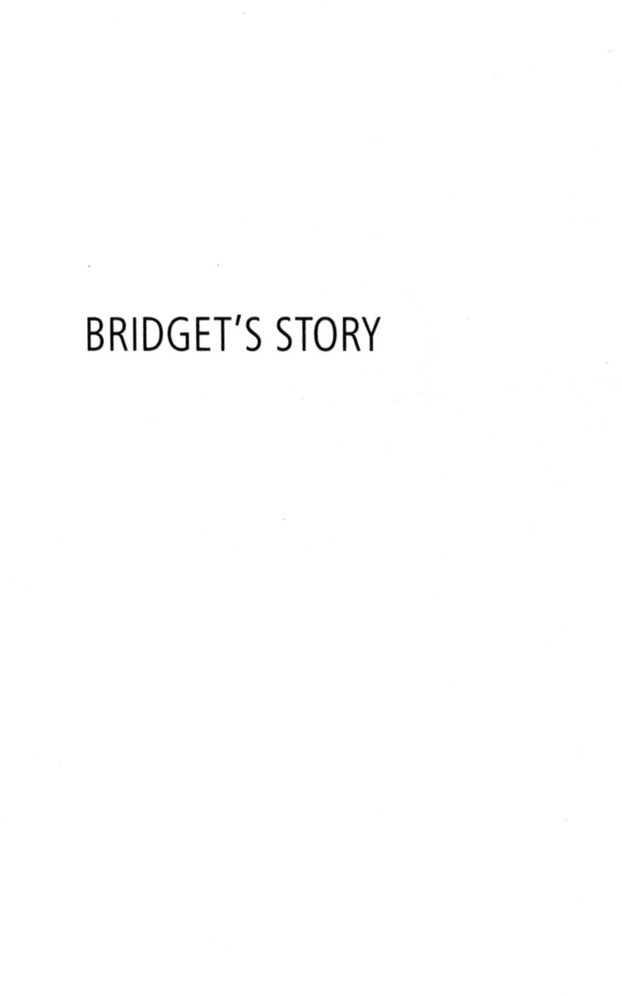

Getting Old And Loving It

I have wrinkles and grey hair, which isn't great on the physical level. I would love to have been blessed with a First Nation's blood, to have their creamy complexions that never seem to age. The grandmothers look younger than I do. As a European I am blessed with the curse of ageing un-elegantly, though living without mirrors helps to keep the importance of how I look in its rightful place, which is at the bottom of the totem pole.

I am 33 and life just keeps getting better and better. I am fitter and stronger than I have ever been. Hiking everyday so Jack can discover the wilderness, the physical chores of hauling wood and water, and gardening in the summer, all keep my body strong and able, and I seem to thrive on all the pure fresh air. All this balances my mind, and gives my soul a chance to be felt and heard. Which makes me feel great. Happily gone is the neurosis of caring what others think and how they perceive me, all the boring body image issues. Bye, bye. What a waste of time.

I know for certain that on the day I die those issues won't be important, so instead I appreciate life. I am sitting here breathing in and out, and for that I am truly grateful. Today is a gift, and if this is all I have gained from living up here it is enough, because it has freed me from fear. The fear to try. The fear of making a mistake. The fear of making a fool of myself. The fear of not being popular. The fear of being fat. The fear of being different. The fear of being myself. I am free and life is great.

My First Moose Hunting Experience

My girlfriend Sandy and I went out early one autumn day. Not very long into the day I spotted a bull moose. It was beautiful in only the way a huge, gangly, long-legged, big-nosed, wild animal can be. We stalked it for about one and half-hours until we were in a good shooting position, and then my girlfriend shot it. After what seemed like a lifetime it dropped to the ground, as if suddenly overwhelmed by a desire to sleep. We walked to where it lay and found it dead, then went and recruited a big, strong Dorian.

What has never left me is that I saw it when it was alive and knew it for about one and a half hours before we killed it. I then saw it dead, helped to dress it and to carry it out of the bush. I had an overwhelming urge to thank it and say good-bye, so that is what I did. We took it home and hung it in quarters for a week and then we butchered it, wrapped it and froze it. Because of all this, when it came to the first meal I couldn't eat it. I carried a large burden of guilt securely on my shoulders.

But I couldn't waste the meat, not after taking an animal's life. I talked to some First Nations people, who were very clear that gratefulness rather than guilt should accompany any deliberate act of killing an animal for food. They said that the animal gave itself to feed and nourish me, that I must respect that and take responsibility for taking it's life by using all that it gave me.

I ate it and enjoyed the taste and nourishment it gave me and today I can still see that moose as if I were looking straight at it.

Because of this experience I now believe I am responsible for whatever meat I am eating. My sister thinks killing wild animals for meat is cruel. For me buying meat when I don't know the conditions in which the animal has died is questionable at the very least. We give thanks every single time we eat game we have killed and it is amazing how difficult we find it. At first we felt stupid. Imagine that, feeling stupid for saying how grateful we are to have a plate full of food. Moose are magnificent animals and that first one in particular was young and very beautiful. Mahsi cho. Thank you.

Walking To Work While Pregnant

While I was pregnant I would walk to work and something great would happen every day. An hour's walk would take me down through the forest, across and along the frozen river and through town to the office. I would always hope to see wildlife, but in the winter darkness even the animals seemed to know how rude it is to have to get up before it's light. The highlight for me would be crossing the river, which is flanked by hills and mountains. Down river was a whole wilderness I hadn't as yet explored fully, up river was Dawson City with all its stories, adventures and tragedies.

I couldn't wait to get through the forest because after the trees came the river. My joy I think was because I realised I was no longer fearful of being on my own, outside, in the dark, in the woods. When I was a child and young adult I was scared of the dark, I was scared of the woods and I was scared of being on my own. So much so that I used to sleep with a knife under my pillow. I don't know exactly how and when it happened, but now I am no longer afraid.

I would begin to cross the river but halfway would have

to stop so that I could really be in my surroundings, and hear them. The river would try and tell me that I was not safe, the mountain would look down at me succumbing to its greatness, the wind would touch my skin and exhilarate me and the silence would try to slow down my overactive thoughts. There would often be an open part of the river with dark water still running and it was so thrilling, walking that close to danger. I loved the rush of excitement.

To me it was absolutely amazing that this was how I got to work, walking with nature most of the way. Almost unconsciously I would acknowledge her with gratitude and respect. It felt natural, as if I was tapping into an inner self we all must have had hundreds of years ago, which guided us and told us how to behave.

Living In The Yukon

I am a lazy person by nature and will only work when I absolutely have to, yet I get huge enjoyment out of working or accomplishing something. It makes me feel alive, a feeling I welcome into my heart. I skedaddled up here so quickly because I knew it would push me, make me struggle and to live. And a struggle it is.

In this way of life nothing ever goes to plan. If it's easy or simple, wait five minutes and the situation will change. You have to get used to things going wrong all the time and dealing with it. I spent my first 20 odd years trying to make life as easy as possible, and when things went wrong it felt like a catastrophe. Yet it's when things go wrong that I push myself, my boundaries, my beliefs and my fears. I'm not so focused now on trying to prevent things from going wrong, because things do whether it's my fault or someone else's. It doesn't matter, because it isn't a catastrophe, it's life.

One of the things I worried about most before I came to the Yukon was death. I couldn't believe that we were alive only then to die. I couldn't deal with the thought of being alone at the end or ceasing to exist. Because I now live somewhere where it takes a week to get to, I face death head on, everywhere and every day. I've never been closer to it, and animals and people die here regularly. Since we arrived there has been one murder, three suicides, four horrible accidental deaths and several natural deaths of people in the community and people close to me. We have killed caribou and moose, not to mention the wildfowl and hares that have found their way to our table. None of this just happens and is then ignored, it is with us because of all of this harshness and reality. As the raven sits in the tree watching me, I have been forced to acknowledge and live with death. Life is truly a gift.

Looking back over our trip it seems symbolic that it was 1999 when we started our journey into a new life. How great to have spent the last year of a century travelling and searching for a life, and then to find it at the start of a new century. It didn't really mean anything to us at the time, though perhaps all the hype leading up to the turn of the millennium sent some ideas to our unconscious. Which then came to us as dreams. And I guess they were pretty powerful dreams, because we appear to still be in them.

There are many reasons why we chose to do what we did and to live how we live, all of them sprouting from a feeling of discontentment. But because I listened to it - I couldn't really ignore it, it was so loud - I have arrived here, exactly where I need to be, to learn what I want to learn and to be content. I haven't been able to escape me, but instead I am now someone I don't want to escape from.

Being with Jack has added a whole new dimension to living here. We hear about my cousins' children the same age going swimming and having music lessons, and we sometimes doubt whether we are giving Jack the best environment. But we reassure ourselves by looking at how sound, stable and wise some of our neighbours are who were brought up in the bush. Their social skills are impeccable, even if they are a little shy, and they have a good philosophy on life. Some of their siblings have left to live in cities in the south, and they seem to be doing really well. So we will be staying here, for now at least, because it feels as though the adventure of life is only just beginning. Jack is definitely just beginning.

The First Nations people of the Yukon believe that our lives are a story. At the end, what will your story be?

FACTS ABOUT CANADA'S YUKON TERRITORY

In the Athapaskan language, the word "Yukon" means "the great river" or "big river." At 3,600 kilometres (2,300 mi.), the Yukon River is the fourth longest river in North America; the fifth largest in water flow and the last major river on the continent to be explored in the 1800s The Yukon Territory is 483,450 square kilometres (186,661 sq. mi.) big. That's larger than the State of California and larger than Belgium, Denmark, Germany and the Netherlands combined.

Barren ground caribou: 185,000
Moose: 50,000
People: 31,881
Mountain sheep: 25,000
Grizzly bears: 10,000
Black bears: 7,000
Birds: 254 (species)
Fish: 38 (species)

The human population of Yukon was higher in 1898 than it is now. Dawson City alone reached a population of over 30,000 at the height of the Klondike Gold Rush. The population of Whitehorse, the current capital of Yukon, was 23,133 in 1993.

A RICH CULTURAL HERITAGE

Yukon First Nations people include the Southern and Northern Tutchone, Tlingit, Tagish, Kaska, Tanana, Han and Gwitchin people. The Inuvialuit peoples' traditional hunting grounds include the northern Yukon. The Athapaskan language group is shared by the Tutchone, Tagish, Kaska, Tanana, Han and Gwitchin people the largest group of Athapaskans today are the Navajo people in the southwestern United States.

RIBBONS OF HIGHWAY

There are 4,734.8 kilometres (2,942.2 mi.) of highway in Yukon, including some of the most spectacular and unusual drives in the world. The Dempster Highway, the only public road in Canada to cross the Arctic Circle, is an astonishing drive through Arctic tundra. The Klondike Highway roughly follows the route used by the gold seekers of 1898. The Canol Highway is a fabulous trip through pristine wilderness, past whitewater rivers and blue-green lakes.

MOUNTAINS AND MORE MOUNTAINS

The St. Elias Mountains in Kluane National Park are the youngest mountains in Canada and also the highest. There are more than 20 summits over 4,200 meters (14,000 ft.), the largest accumulation on the continent. Overseeing these lofty peaks is Mount Logan, Canada's highest mountain at 5,959 metres (19,551 ft.), and one of the world's largest massifs. And they're still growing a seismograph in the Visitor Reception Centre at Haines Junction records the hundreds of small tremors that occur every year, pushing the St. Elias Mountains ever skyward.

THE ICE QUEEN

Between the rock massifs of the St. Elias Mountains is one of the largest non-polar icefields in the world. Huge valley glaciers fill the gulfs between the peaks; the Hubbard Glacier is 112 kilometres (70 mi.) long, the Lowell Glacier is 72 kilometres (45 mi.) long and these glaciers may be 1.6 kilometres (1 mi.) thick in parts. These glaciers make their own weather, scour away tons of rock every day, dam rivers and create lakes.

GALLOPING GLACIERS

The Steele Glacier in Kluane National Park surged for several months in 1966-67, moving over 1.5 billion tons of ice at a rate of up to 15 metres (50 ft.) per day. Surging valley glaciers are not uncommon in Kluane, where the Lowell Glacier has a history of galloping, blocking the Alsek River and forming a lake. There are more than 2,000 glaciers in Kluane National Park including valley glaciers, hanging glaciers, cirque glaciers and rock glaciers.

UNESCO WORLD HERITAGE SITE

One of the Yukon's great treasures, Kluane National Park, is a designated UNESCO World Heritage Site. It contains the wonders of the St. Elias Mountains and its icefields, glacial lakes, wild rivers and pristine forests. Interpretive trails and exhibits will introduce you to the wonders of one of North America's most awe-inspiring wilderness preserves.

CANADIAN HERITAGE RIVERS

The Alsek and the Thirty-Mile are both Canadian Heritage Rivers, and the Bonnet Plume has been nominated for this special status. The Thirty-Mile rushes from lower Lake Laberge, while the Alsek River courses through Kluane National Park past calving glaciers and awesome mountain scenery. The Bonnet Plume is loved by canoeists from around the world for its challenging whitewater and outstanding wilderness setting.

NORTHERN FESTIVALS

Northern festivals are times of enthusiasm and release for Yukoners. Visit Yukon during the Yukon Sourdough Rendezvous, Dawson Discovery Days, Klondike Outhouse Races, Yukon International Storytelling Festival, Yukon Quest Dog Sled Race, Frostbite Music Festival or Dawson City Music Festival. See for yourself what the fuss is all about!

LAND OF THE MIDNIGHT SUN

On June 21, summer solstice, the sun never sets in some parts of Yukon. All over the Territory you can read a book outdoors all night. The midnight sun makes for long summer days, and wondrous carmine and magenta skyscapes that last for hours, rather than minutes.

THE WORLD'S SMALLEST DESERT

The Carcross Desert is affectionately known as the world's smallest desert. The dry climate and wind conditions have created sand dunes and forced special vegetation to adapt to the surroundings. This pocket desert is a popular tourist attraction.

RARE MINERALS

More than 30 types of rare phosphate minerals have been discovered in the Blow River area. Many of these minerals are new to science. The exceptionally rare lazulite crystals gave Yukon its official gemstone. Samples of these minerals are on display in Whitehorse.

THE BLUE FISH CAVES

The Blue Fish Caves on the Bluefish River in the northern Yukon contain the earliest evidence of human habitation in North America. Today, some experts believe humans have lived in this region for more than 14,000 years.

SOURDOUGHS AND CHEECHAKOS

Sourdough (a fermenting mixture of flour, water, and a pinch of sugar and rice) hung in a kettle over the wood stove of many Yukoners. It was used as a starter to make delicious sourdough bread. "Sourdough" became the word used to describe a Yukon old-timer. A Cheechako, on the other hand, is a "greenhorn" or newcomer to Yukon. There's only one way for a cheechako to become a sourdough: he or she must watch the river freeze in the fall and break into grinding pieces in the spring. The term "sourdough" was immortalized in Robert Service's first collection of verse, "Songs of the Sourdough."

SNOW IN SUMMER?

Not likely. The Yukon has warm, sun-rich summers with average temperatures in July of 14 to 16°C (57 to 60°F), and highs that can reach 35°C (95°F). The average temperature in January is between -18 and -25°C (0 and -15°F), though lows can reach -55°C (-58°F). Most of Yukon's climate is semi-arid, so snow and rainfall are light; on average there's just 26.8 centimetres (10.5 in.) of precipitation a year in Whitehorse, the capital.

SORRY, NO IGLOOS

The igloo is an ancestral dwelling for Canada's Inuit peoples. Although the Inuvialuit have traditional territory in the northern Yukon, they do not live in igloos there. The skin tent was the ancestral shelter for Yukon First Nations peoples.

THE SOUND OF LIGHT

The Northern Lights, or Aurora Borealis, are caused by huge explosions on the surface of the sun that send out streams of charged particles that interact with the Earth's upper atmosphere. These reactions occur 96 to 128 kilometres (60 to 80 mi.) above the Earth's surface.

For further information on the Yukon, go to:
www.touryukon.com

If you are interested in visiting the Yukon or would like to find out further details on what you can do when there, we recommend that you contact the tour operators on the following pages.

FrontierCanada

This is a book about adventure. It tells the story of an English couple who gave up their comfortable life in Cornwall to face the challenges and hardship of creating a life in the Yukon. It is a tale of freedom, the open road and limitless horizons. And it is a book about an extraordinary corner of an incredible country.

We specialise in tailor-made holidays for the independent traveller across the whole of Canada. We know and love the Yukon, Dawson City and the Top of the World Highway. We also know and love Canada's ancient rainforests and Pacific beaches, snow-capped Rockies and glacial lakes, and we too love its vastness and its tranquillity.

Hire a motorhome or car, and stay in backcountry cabins or luxury hotels. Canoe, raft, ride horses or mountain bikes, skim the ocean waves among the orcas, or peep down from your hide at a feeding grizzly bear. Hike through valley floors and along mountain peaks. Whatever you chose, we can arrange it.

But be warned. Just like the heroes of this book, you might never want to leave!

Call the specialists on 020 8776 8709 or visit our website:

www.frontier-canada.co.uk

THE GOOD LIFE

STARTS HERE

telephone: 0845 644 3545

mail-mail@1stclassholidays.com **Internet-www.1stclassholidays.com**

Specialists in Service

ATOL Protected: 5421

Enjoy the Yukon's majestic scenery both in summer and winter. Windows on the Wild has the largest collection of holidays to the Yukon.

Winter Holidays - dog sledding, northern lights, snow shoeing, cross country skiing, snowmobiling and tobogganing.

Summer Holidays - fishing, bear viewing, hiking the Chilkoot Trail, touring, kayaking, canoeing some of the Yukon's great rivers such as the Yukon and Big Salmon and rafting the Tatshenshini River.

Phone 0208 742 1556 www.windowsonthewild.com
Fax 0208 742 4331 sales@windowsonthewild.com

ATOL Protected: 2966

About Eye Books

Eye books is a young, dynamic publishing company that likes to break the rules. Our independence allows us to publish books which challenge the way people see things. It also means that we can offer new authors a platform from which they can shine their light and encourage others to do the same.

To date we have published 30 books that cover a number of genres including Travel, Biography, Adventure and History. Many of our books are experience driven. All of them are inspirational and life-affirming.

Frigid Women, for example, tells the story of the world-record making first all female expedition to the North Pole. A fifty year-old mother of three who had recently recovered from a mastectomy, and her daughter are the authors neither had ever written a book before. Sue Riches is now both author and highly sought after motivational speaker.

We also publish thematic anthologies, such as The Tales from Heaven and Hell series, for those who prefer the short story format. Here everyone has the chance to get their stories published and win prizes such as flights to any destination in the world.

And here's what makes us really different: As well as publishing books, Eye Books has set up a club for like-minded people and is in the process of developing a number of initiatives and services for its community of members. After all, the more you put into life, the more you get out of it.

Please visit www.eye-books.com for further information.

New Titles by Eye Books

Riding The Outlaw Trail - Simon Casson
ISBN: 1 903070 228

Desert Governess - Phyllis Ellis
ISBN: 1 903070 015

The Last Of The Nomads - W. J. Peasley
ISBN: 1 903070 325

First Contact - Mark Anstice
ISBN: 1 903070 260

All Will Be Well - Michael Meegan
ISBN: 1 903070 279

Special Offa - Bob Bibby
ISBN: 1 903070 287

Further Travellers' Tales From Heaven And Hell - Various
ISBN: 1 903070 112

Green Oranges On Lion Mountain - Emily Joy
ISBN: 1 903070 295

Baghdad Business School - Heyrick Bond-Gunning
ISBN: 1 903070 333

The Con Artist Handbook - Joel Levy
ISBN: 1 903070 341

The Forensics Handbook - Pete Moore
ISBN: 1 903070 35X

Book Microsites

If you are interested in finding out more about this book please visit the author's website or our book microsite:

www.dorianamos.com

www.eye-books.com/thegoodlife/home.htm

We have also created microsites for a number of our other new books including:

Riding The Outlaw Trail
Desert Governess
The Last of the Nomads
Special Offa
No Socks No Sex
Baghdad Business School

For details on these sites and others which we are developing please visit our main website:

www.eye-books.com

Special Offers and Promotions

We are offering our club members and people who have read this book the opportunity to take advantage of promotions on our other books by buying direct from us.

For information on these special offers please visit the following page of our website:

www.eye-books.com/promotions.htm